Staying Awake

A True Story of Life in Death

Thomas A. Lukenbill

Park East Press

Printed in the United States of America.

For information address:

Park East Press
The Graybar Building
420 Lexington Avenue, Suite 300
New York, NY 10170

Library of Congress Cataloging-in-Publication Data

Lukenbill, Thomas A.

Staying Awake/Thomas A. Lukenbill

Library of Congress Control Number: 2011924572

p. cm.

ISBN: 978-1-935764-20-5

10 9 8 7 6 5 4 3 2 1

Acknowledgments

First and foremost, a very special thank you to God, the universe, or whoever was in charge that gifted me with this amazing experience. It was truly life changing. To my loving parents that gave me life, you both were such pillars in my life. To my family and friends that have stood by me through this whole process, I can't say thank you enough to let you all know how much I appreciate the support I received from all of you. I refrain from listing names because I don't want to leave anyone out. A big thank you once again to everyone that has come in contact with me over the years. Thanks for the friendships and support.

Prologue

Knowing death as a friendly, even loving presence was as odd a concept to me as being a vegetarian while growing up on a cattle farm. Like many youths, I had wrestled with the concept of death throughout my childhood and adolescence. I did not come to understand it, and in fact came to fear it more and more.

During this time, I once asked God to save my mother after she'd suffered a stroke. When she indeed survived and recovered, I felt I might have gained a type of influence over death. Yet then, soon after, my father died.

I grieved for my father, accepting the inevitability of a parent's death as we all must, but I did not shake the fear of and contempt for death itself. I felt death's dark presence lurking behind me at every turn, keeping a distance, just waiting. All the same, I did what I could to move on and give my attention to other important aspects of life, to relationships, career, and new experiences.

Then one day death returned: my mother was in the hospital. The terrifying circumstances left me obliged to decide her fate. This time, Death has won, I thought. I not only could not save her, I had no idea how to save her. I could only decide when she would die. Death had put me at its service.

But there the story does not end. Rather, the time of my mother's death was what I see now as a crucial waypoint of an unfolding spiritual journey, the distinct path of which I only now have come to discern more clearly. For it was while my mother lay dying that I discovered death is but an angel of deliverance. I was allowed to accompany my mother to the other side. I held death's hand, felt its warm caress, and then I let go. Or I was let go.

Admittedly, I did not know then what was happening, and I resisted assigning any larger meaning to my experience. However, when I returned to life, to my life, all fear of death was gone. Since that time of death and dying, I have never felt more at peace among the living. I have decided to stay here, and to stay awake.

Chapter One

Fight or Flight

I train horses. When faced with fear, horses react in two different ways—the well known "fight or flight" response. When over time a horse comes to understand what you are trying to accomplish as a trainer, the horse's learning capabilities accelerate and the training process itself becomes very smooth.

When I was very young, death came knocking at my door. It was in the form of my mother falling ill and nearly dying. If she had died then, my world would have been turned upside down. A fear of her death and of death itself began to build inside me. Fortunately, my mother recovered. With this reprieve, my inner fears subsided.

Yet, a year and a half later, death showed up at my family's doorstep once again. Without warning, my father was ripped from my life. Now, the fear of death within me at thirteen years of age was more than I could handle. Death was a reality, and it was something I now had to face. In my family death was not discussed openly, and so the questions I had in my head about my father's death could only fester.

Similar to a fearful horse, I had two options at this early stage in my life: I could either fight through my fear of death and face it, or choose to run as fast as I could and hide from it. I chose the latter. Death now had a grip on me and my life on a very deep level. I could not run fast enough.

When still a youth and riding atop a very strong and powerful horse through the hills on our 1,000-acre ranch in North Dakota, I felt as though the faster I rode, the further I would get from death's grip. Indeed, such frantic effort would later turn me into a workaholic. Once an adult, I felt that if I kept myself busy, the fear that haunted me could be kept locked away inside my subconscious, in a trunk of sorts, never to resurface. The key to that trunk was long gone, and there was no way I wanted to unlock that container of death.

I had always tried to stay one step ahead of death, which I felt was right on my heels. Even before death had entered my life as a young child, I would lie in my bed late at night wondering who was talking in my room. The old cliché "I hear voices" was something that I experienced at a very young age. Some may say that I was crazy; others might say it was my imagination. All I knew was what I heard at the time, and that it was real. There were many nights when there was so much chatter, I resorted to turning on a small stereo system and praying that I would fall asleep before the record finished. It didn't necessarily scare me to hear the voices; all I questioned was who was I hearing.

The voices continued on for years, until they became a normal part of my everyday life. It still happens to this day, and I enjoy the experience of really paying attention in order to try to decipher what the voices are communicating to me. Is it angels having a conversation around me, or some other strong spiritual influence in my life?

Extraordinary occurrences have been a constant in my life. As best I remember, the very first time that something quite remarkable happened was a few years after my father's death. As I was sitting at our large dining table in the kitchen, I caught a glimpse of a figure coming down the hallway from the bedroom area and making its way into the living room. This figure was someone I recognized but hadn't seen in a couple of years. Excited, but a little hesitant, I got up from the table and wandered around the corner to have a glimpse into the living room. I saw a man resembling my father sitting in his favorite black recliner.

The sight took my breath away, and I stood motionless in the hallway. I knew at that point that my life was going to be a series of unexplained events. I never discussed with my siblings this encounter with my father. At the time, I felt as though I didn't want to upset anyone, nor did I want anyone to think that I was crazy. I didn't need anyone telling me what I did or didn't see.

I wanted to embrace my father as I stood staring at his spirit body. But all I could really do was stand and gaze at him with amazement. How and why was this happening? Was it because I was running so fast to escape from the fear of death? Was it because the fear or questions that I had concerning death were now going to be slowly answered? Not knowing, at that young age, that I could have had a conversation with him, I watched him slowly get up from his black recliner and walk into what seemed to be thin air. For years I cherished that moment, not knowing that more such experiences were to come.

Ten years later, I was muddling my way through life. It was a beautiful summer evening when I made my way to bed. The night air was crisp, and I had left my bedroom window and drapes open. The street light from the cul-de-sac that I lived on lit up my room just enough to enjoy the summer breezes but not enough to keep me awake. Suddenly, I was awakened by the feeling of somebody sitting at the end of my bed. I sat up and rubbed my eyes and saw a figure sitting on the foot of my bed. Once again, I stared at the familiar figure. I instantly knew by his broad shoulders and dark hair that my father had returned from the other side to visit me.

I'd reached a point in my life where I was required to deal with some challenges. I had been spending a lot of time praying for validation that I had chosen the right thing for my life. My father slowly stood; when he did I felt the foot of the bed rise. He walked around and put his hand on my forehead. "Everything is going to be fine, son," he said.

His touch from that evening has been with me since that day. The energy that came from him was something I needed to get through the difficult time in my life. Not wanting him to leave, I watched him slowly back away from my bed and disappear once again into thin air, as if he had backed into and through my wall.

Stunned by what had just happened, I turned on the lamp, got up, went into my roommate's room, and shook him awake.

"Whoa, man, you startled me," he said. "What's going on?"

"I need to ask you a simple question," I said. "Were you just sitting on the foot of my bed?"

"No, man, you must've been dreaming. I've been sleeping. Why do you ask?"

"No reason," I said. "You're right, I must've been dreaming."

I went into the kitchen and got a glass of milk. I turned from the refrigerator to look at a photograph of my mother and father that was sitting on a window ledge. "Thanks for the visit, Dad," I said. "Your words meant a lot."

Back in bed, I tossed for hours before falling asleep. My father visited me from the other side. With that thought, I prayed myself to sleep.

At sunrise, I got up to start the day. My roommate joined me a few minutes later in the kitchen. "I'm still wondering why you woke me up last night, thinking I was in your room," he said. "That's not like you, Tom."

"Sorry," I said. "I must've been having a heck of a dream."

To this day, I believe everything my father said to me that night. I continued through life knowing what was supposed to happen was going to happen.

Trying not to fight what life places before us is a challenge, to say the least. However, I've learned that challenges in life produce learning experiences that enable us to grow.

As we move through life, we phase in and out of situations just as we may move in and out of different homes. A few years later, after leaving the home in which my father had made his appearance, I began renting from some friends. The lease stipulated that rather than pay rent, I was to fix up and maintain the home. It was a good deal for me, as I've always enjoyed renovating something that is run down or broken and bringing it back to life.

Before moving in, I painted the rooms. The last room I painted was the back bedroom. I'll never forget what happened that day, as this memory is as clear today as it was years ago. As I started painting, I got an eerie feeling that somebody was watching me. I removed the roller from the cinderblock wall and turned around. No one was there. My only companion in the house was the cat. I laughed at myself and began rolling fresh paint on the wall. Then something happened that made the hair on the back of my neck stand up.

I turned around quickly to see if anyone was watching me. Again, no one was there. I took a deep breath and tried to shake it off and went back to my painting. A moment later, something came so close that I could feel its breath on my neck. I dropped the roller in the pan, then ran out of the room and slammed the door behind me.

What was happening? Who or what was in the back bedroom? I grabbed the cordless phone in the kitchen and headed to the front door. I called the owner and told her what had happened in the back room. "I'm sorry, but I'm no longer interested in renting," I said.

Why was this making me so nervous? I had seen and heard many things in the past that were unexplainable. So why was this situation so different?

"Oh, you're one of those," the lady who owned the home said. I didn't quite understand what she was saying at the moment, but she understood what I was feeling. She then explained to me how she had bought the house from a bank. The previous homeowner had passed away in that back bedroom. He'd had no living relatives and was not found for weeks. I now understood why I was having those feelings in that back bedroom. The previous homeowner's spirit had not left the room, as he had no idea he had passed away. The spirit was very angry that someone was in his home, repainting it.

Because I had had no vision of the deceased previous owner, the fact that he was trying to communicate with me about his concerns really threw me for a loop. Maybe if I would have seen the face attached to that energy, it wouldn't have scared me so much. I proceeded to move out of that home as quickly as I had moved in and was on to my next place of residence.

Training horses puts you in contact with many people and into varied situations. A customer once expressed interest in acquiring a new horse for his daughter, and I was soon in the Midwest looking for one. The father and I flew to our destination and drove a rental car to a ranch where we had an appointment. After examining the horse, we decided it was not the right one for his daughter. Disappointed, we nonetheless continued with our hopes of finding the right horse on that trip.

An inexplicable impulse had me turning into the driveway of a ranch that I spotted along the road. We got out of the car and proceeded to the barn to question the ranch owner if there were any horses for sale on this property. It turned out he did have a few for sale and proceeded to take us into the barn to show us.

I will never forget what happened when the ranch owner opened a stall door to show us a large buckskin gelding. As the door was opened, I noticed the horse had been exercised and was cooling off while loosely tied to the stall wall. As I looked through the stall door, the gelding turned his head and looked at me. In the background behind him there was a lightly cast shadow that resembled a world champion show photography backdrop. Why was I seeing this horse with a backdrop behind him? Was something in the universe trying to show me that this horse was going to be my first world champion?

Not questioning what I had seen, I tried to hold back my excitement and told my customer this was the horse that we needed. He asked how I knew without riding him, and I responded by saying, "I just know." He requested that I ride the horse and try it out. I insisted I didn't need to. The father looked at me, quite confused, and said that he wasn't comfortable purchasing the horse unless I rode him and tested him out. I giggled inside and responded by saying, "No problem, I will give him a test ride."

While test riding the horse, I didn't request that the animal perform anything complicated. I had just been shown by some force or energy that if I believed in myself and this animal enough, then he was going to be my first world champion. We made the purchase and had the horse shipped back to the equestrian center where I worked at the time. I had nine months to gain the horse's trust before we were to head off to my first world championship show.

After two long days traveling to the world show, we arrived with much anticipation. I was very excited to compete. Notwithstanding the vision I'd had nine months ago, I still had to believe in myself and my animal to compete at top form and win a world title. Not only did I win one world title, but I won two, including two reserve world titles. Winning the world titles was a goal that I had had when I became a horse trainer and something that I had dreamt about for many years. I felt as if I was floating on air when my name was called as world champion.

I could have dismissed the vision that I had experienced nine months earlier and chalked it up as simply a coincidence. Yet I have always chosen to stay alert and aware of what the universe has to share with me. Sometimes things in our lives get in our way and we miss these small details.

Life leads us down many paths, and my job training horses took me across the United States from one coast to the other. One year after competing on the East Coast for a year-end championship, I found myself driving back to the West Coast in the month of December. Stopping at one of our night layovers, we quickly settled in for an early evening. With the horses resting in their stalls, I was soon in bed myself. I was very tired from the long drive and fell asleep rather quickly.

The guest house in which I was staying was above the garage with a long hallway leading to the main house. The bed was positioned in a way so that I could see the long hallway to the main house. For some odd reason, I did not feel the need to shut the door that evening when I went to bed.

After sleeping for a few hours, I was jolted from a deep sleep. I saw a vision of a woman not walking, but floating down the hallway to me. I was frozen for a moment. My eyes were fixed on her, trying to recognize her. The fear that entered my body at that moment was more than I could handle. I jumped out of bed and grabbed my clothes and bag and ran quickly down the stairs and into the apartment in which my assistant was staying. I woke her up and insisted we leave the property now.

To my surprise, she agreed. After we left, she explained to me that she had had something unusual happen to her while trying to fall asleep. She had felt an arm slide under her neck while it was resting on the pillow and slowly try to sit her upright in bed. The experience made her a little nervous and uneasy, and she was more than happy to leave the guest house and continue traveling back home.

The following summer I decided to take a trip to see my sister, who resides in Minnesota. I was so looking forward to having a week off to finally relax at their lake house. The four-hour flight to their home seemed very short. I was picked up at the airport, and we had an additional four-hour drive to my sister's home. It was around midnight when we arrived, and we quietly entered the home, not wanting to wake up my sister's husband or her daughter.

I had never been to their home, and upon entering I got a weird feeling that someone else was in the home besides her family. I walked around quietly, looking at the home and not saying anything to my sister. She thought that was rather odd, but thought I was just being quiet so as not to wake up her family. We chatted for a few minutes and decided to call it a night. I struggled to fall asleep that evening as I was trying to figure out what I was feeling in her home.

Morning broke, and within a few moments we all were up and sitting around the breakfast table. While breakfast was being made, my sister, her daughter and I were catching up with one another's lives. My eyes began to focus on the spiral staircase that led to the basement. There was something lingering in that space. I tried to keep myself distracted and not focus on what was occurring on the spiral staircase. Then abruptly I said, "Oh, Eleanor, it will be just fine."

My sister looked at me quite strangely, and before she could say anything, I asked my niece to go down and get a coloring book so we could color. My sister knew what I was up to and asked her daughter to go get her favorite coloring book. Once my niece was gone, I explained to my sister and her husband that something or someone was in this home and was hovering in the area of the spiral staircase.

My sister asked her husband to run down to the safe and get the deed of the home to identify who the previous homeowners were. To no one's surprise, the owner's name on the deed was "Elaine." That was close enough for me. I asked my sister if she had ever known an Elaine, and she said no. I reassured my sister and her family that Elaine was a kind spirit and there was nothing to fear.

Later that day we decided to go for a pontoon ride. With my sister's husband at the wheel and the rest of us on the front portion of the pontoon, we set sail for a nice evening on the lake. The cool breeze coming off the lake had all of us bundled up in blankets. The pontoon ride was very enjoyable, and after an hour we headed back to the house.

On rounding the cove and seeing their house from a distance, to my surprise there was a vision of a woman standing in the large picture window facing the lake. Looking closer, I noticed she was a smaller-framed woman with grayish hair. I looked over at my sister, and she knew that something had caught my eye. I watched the vision of this woman continue to stare at the lake. As we pulled up to the dock, the woman began to fade into the background of the house. After my niece had gone to bed, my sister and I had a conversation about this vision that I had experienced.

My sister was so intrigued with my story that a few days later, after I had gone home, she took a drive to the home of Elaine's daughter. She told the daughter of my experience with Elaine, picking up her energy in the spiral staircase and later seeing her in the picture window staring at the lake.

Elaine's daughter was very excited to hear about it. She informed my sister that the spiral staircase used to be an elevator that would carry her mother from the first floor to the second floor. For the last few years of her life, her mother was confined to a wheelchair and would use the elevator many times a day. She also would sit in front of the picture window and stare at the lake for hours. My sister was then shown a picture of the home's former owner. It was exactly how I had described "Elaine" to her. Driving back to her home, my sister got a sense of peace and closure, knowing there was a wonderful energy of someone who was still making herself present in their home.

Chapter Two

In All That You Do

I awoke to another beautiful California morning, to a day promising work in the surrounding green hills amid early spring flowers under non-stop sunshine. As I readied for a day at the barn with my friends—fifteen horses calling to be exercised and ridden—I ran through the checklist in my mind. I mechanically climbed into the driver's seat, scanning the front seat to make sure I hadn't forgotten anything, and was off.

I passed the familiar streets of quaint little homes, barely noticing them and other sights I had come to take for granted. I wondered how far back I'd actually started to drive through life itself on auto-pilot, everything going fine, the defined lines of life becoming blurred spokes. My mind flitted across various memories, thoughts passing faster than the view out my window, when my cell phone pulled me back to the present moment.

It was my sister, Donna, her voice barely decipherable. She was so shaken and speaking so rapidly I couldn't make out what she was trying to tell me. I had a sinking feeling. I caught my breath and tried to calm her down enough to hear the message: Mom was in the hospital after suffering a stroke. My sister had found her that morning and called the paramedics. I couldn't think about anything other than how fast I could get to Rochester, Minnesota.

I swung the car around at the next intersection and focused on getting back home to throw some clothes in a bag and get on a plane. My mind began to spin with how much needed to be done before I could get to the airport. I wasn't sure what to do first.

I pulled into the driveway, bolted through the door and leapt up the stairs three at a time to get to my bedroom. I threw a suitcase down on the bed and began tossing my usual shorts and t-shirts in as though Minnesota was going to be enjoying the balmy 75-degree weather we were experiencing in Chino Hills that day. It dawned on me that this attire wasn't going to do it.

I picked up the phone and asked a friend to come over and help me think. She had been a dear friend for the better part of a decade, long enough to sense the urgency in my voice. She graciously offered to come over and help me pack and get me to the airport. Once on the plane, I tried to keep my head from spinning, frequently reminding myself that I had always been capable and dependable. That could not change now.

No more than a hazy memory of the flight itself remains. The drone of engines seemed to segue straight to the moment at the airport in Minneapolis when to my surprise I happened to catch sight of my brother Wes and sister, Karen, who were also trying to make their way to Mom. I was on my way to rent a car at the airport to complete the journey to Rochester's Mayo Clinic, and they were trying to make a connecting flight. I offered them a ride, as the company would have been nice, but since their luggage was already in transit they opted to take their flight. I would again be alone with my thoughts.

I took my belongings and my head fog and hit the road hard and fast—well, eighty. That isn't that fast for California, but for these parts it means one thing: a ticket. To the officer who had stopped me for speeding, I explained the emergency and my desperation to get to the hospital as quickly as possible. He listened while he completed his paperwork. It seemed that I was meant to keep my wits about me and slow down, but I missed that message. I'm probably lucky he didn't impound the car. Anyway, the ticket seemed unimportant. It was only a further delay, and one that I resented.

Some say there are no accidents. I wondered if the delay served a purpose. However, I was in no shape to attempt higher thinking and to piece together life's puzzle. I simply tried to stay as rational as possible.

I didn't yet know what we were up against. Mom had recovered before; maybe it would be the same now. Maybe my sister was overreacting. God, I hoped so. Regardless, I began to prepare for the worst. I was adamant for some reason that I would give my mom thirty days. We could research all possible treatments for her with eight of us there to help. Recovery treatment possibilities must have improved over time. It had been at least twenty-eight years since her last stroke. We would leave no stone unturned. I made a personal commitment that I would not deviate from this thirty-day window and kept driving.

She was in a room on the eighth floor of the hospital, white and sterile walls leading the way. The elevator doors gradually slid open. Time seemed to slow. The ICU hallway was like a white tunnel with an ever-receding end. At last, I reached my mother's door.

There she lay in her bed, a mass of endless tubes running in and out of her body dedicated to making her breathe. The noise was loud, a regimented rasp. It hit me—this was what life support looked like. I stood speechless. Tears began running down my face. In fact, every cell of my being was a watery mess, as though I might simply morph into liquid and wash away. But no such easy escape came. I had to stay solid.

I made my way slowly to her bedside, trying to ignore the tubes that were sustaining her, allowing—or forcing—her to stay with her children. She was conscious, although unable to speak. Our eyes locked and I was swept into a silent space with her. Her gaze told me everything in an instant: she would never be able to fly out to California and visit me again. The reality of the moment broadsided me. All my thoughts seemed to implode. I remembered how dear it was to me that my mom, over seventy, would travel with my sister, Char, and her daughter, Karly, to California to spend time with me. I was instantly filled with remorse at the thought of never having that experience again.

On one of those trips I had taken the three of them to a restaurant that overlooked the Pacific Ocean. The vastness of the water was a sight of wonder for those who were normally landlocked. We finished a leisurely dinner and took a stroll along the beach to enjoy the sunset. I replayed the scene in my mind now, my eyes still fixed on my mom in her hospital bed. It didn't seem that long ago.

I remembered she had sat down on a big rock and took off her shoes and socks. The three of us linked arms and walked backwards into the surf while my niece, just seven or eight at the time, laughed at her elders. We were so carefree and uninhibited. The chilly water on our feet felt invigorating. It had a life of its own, playful, tickling us as the tide moved the lapping water up to us and then pulled it away. We had all enjoyed those moments when we were carefree and together.

I caught myself in the memory and sped through time back to the hospital room. I couldn't imagine what my mother was now feeling. She looked so helpless and fragile, lashed to a bed by tubes and monitors. I held fast to the hope that this would end quickly and Mom would be home soon, would again travel to California. But the hoses and the sound of artificial breathing, the bustling of nurses and hospital personnel, told me otherwise.

I gradually began to assess the situation. I needed to rein in my thoughts and call upon every ounce of strength that I could possibly muster. She had always been strong, had done everything she could to raise her eight children well, and I intended to reassure her that everything was going to be fine, I would take care of everything; I would take care of her.

I looked at her in this state, and the memory of a phone conversation came flooding back. I remembered her mentioning the topic of life support. She confessed that she'd been praying she'd die before she was eighty years old. I knew that she loved spending time with her children and seeing how they had grown to have relationships and families of their own. But she was tired and severely pained with arthritis. She had made me promise that I wouldn't leave her in such a state as this, on life support where she couldn't take care of herself—a condition exactly like this. I had promised to do as she wished, and now she was holding me to my word.

Even though I was the youngest in my family, for some reason I felt like the strongest. Because I had proven to be a rock of stability, my family had come to depend on me, emotionally, in difficult times. Moreover, for the past couple of years I had been working out, losing weight and making myself more physically fit as well. Yet now I was going to need all the physical and emotional endurance I could manage. My mother and everyone here to be with her—my brother, six sisters and my niece—would be counting on me.

I wondered, though, if anyone could really prepare for this situation. Some people are required to be prepared at every moment for anything, such as doctors or military personnel. What do the rest of us do? What, in fact, was my situation? I found myself hanging onto each and every precious breath my mom was taking, searching for answers within the invisible space of air.

I wandered in and out of my mother's room that day consumed with anxiety and helplessness. Was there anything that I could do? My brother and sisters had arrived to help hold vigil; my oldest sister, Barb, and her daughter, Tonya, were scheduled to fly in the next morning from Colorado. The rest of us tried to settle in as best we could, having no idea what tomorrow would bring, let alone the weeks ahead.

Despite the trauma of the stroke, Mom remained aware. Her eyes made contact with us and held fast. That night I sat with her for hours, not wanting to leave her side. She moved restlessly in and out of sleep all night long. From that night on we made sure she never woke up alone in her hospital room.

The next morning we met as a family with the doctors. They relayed the information learned from the CAT scan in small manageable segments so that our troubled minds could comprehend it all clearly. But in a nutshell, the diagnosis and prognosis were not good. She had suffered a massive stroke that would permanently affect her capacity to speak and her ability to walk. However, she was still quite aware and could see and understand everything we were saying to her.

She had suffered a stroke in 1976, though one considered mild compared to what this had done to her brain. Now the doctor placed two CAT scans of our mother's brain side by side on the light board in front of us. I noticed immediately that the brain scan from 1976 carried a black mark on the left side of her brain about the size of a penny. The scan taken the day before revealed a black space on the right side of her brain the size of two softballs. There was no avoiding the fact that this was nothing like the first stroke experience.

My heart sank. I wanted to hold on to the hope that this stroke would be reversible like the last one. Yet blood continued to seep into her brain. If the bleeding would just stop, it would relieve the pressure on her brain so the neurologists wouldn't have to drill a hole in her head. I couldn't bear the thought and prayed this would quickly abate.

I had been in and out of desperate prayer talk since first receiving the news, the muttering that sounds like begging, bartering and making deals to keep the damage minimal, or make it go away altogether. After seeing the CAT scan, I knew that it would take nothing short of a miracle. Christ might have to come down Himself and touch my mom for that kind of healing. My head was spinning when I was jarred back to the present conversation with the doctor.

He wrapped up the meeting, and then the gravity of the situation began to take hold. I watched my sisters as they spoke. Women are the most amazing creatures, the givers of life and makers of wondrous experiences. How often I had observed my mother turn the limited into abundance through a meal, or through an expression of compassion. Although the black cloud was still around me, I felt like I was not alone. I listened to their sweet and nurturing voices and the air began to clear a bit, becoming momentarily lighter, giving me room to breathe without feeling the toxicity of impending disaster and lack of control.

During our stay at the hospital, I'd learned from other family members that Mom had also mentioned to them over the last year that she was ready to die. She really was ready. What about the rest of us? Were we ready for her to pass on? She was adamant about not wanting to live out the rest of her days at a nursing home.

I suggested to all then that each family member have some time alone with Mom to express their love and to let her know whatever they needed to say to make their peace. We all agreed that with Mom still aware, we would take turns the next day to spend time with her alone to reassure her that we were all okay and that we loved her. The desire to relieve her of any suffering was most important. It was time to let her know that she was a blessing to us, that she would live on fondly in our hearts.

The meeting dwindled to a close during that first full day at the hospital. We all filed out of the waiting room and headed somberly in different directions. I attempted to regain some strength. I tried to sleep that night with my head resting on Mom's bed, gently touching her hand. I woke to the slightest movement that she made to make sure that she was all right. I tried to calm myself with the knowledge that there were professional ICU nurses just six feet away checking on her vital signs constantly, available nonstop, and I felt reassured at the thought.

I couldn't pretend to understand what was happening. The essentials were obvious, but a strange heaviness was beginning to gather within me. I was grateful for my large family; they brought many blessings. One of them was assuring that Mother would almost never be alone in her hospital room. Still, there was so much to grasp. The doctors were keeping us all well informed, but we still found ourselves waiting. Waiting for the wisdom to know what needed to be done. My brother, the quiet type, asked if I would take over as spokesman for the family. I had doubts that I could carry the responsibility, but I knew I had to be strong.

Just as Mom was fighting for life, I became aware that I was fighting an inner battle of my own. How could I stand strong for the rest of the family when I felt like I was going to drown at any moment? Throughout the day they came to me for support. I believe that for the most part they tried to offer their encouragement, but I was too burdened with self-imposed responsibility to benefit from it fully. All day I heard variations of, "We are so glad that you're here, Tom. We wouldn't know what to do without you here," and "You are the rock of the family." They meant well, but with every validation of confidence, the decisions to be made appeared more enormous.

Chapter Three

Heaven's Protection

As a gift of fate, we found that the bleeding in her brain subsided on its own during the second night. I stayed with Mom again that night. I remember finding myself mesmerized by her. She had meant so much to all of us in her own special way. She had taught me to be independent, strong and loving all at the same time. She had encouraged me to work out any situation I found myself in, taught me to never quit no matter how much I wanted to and to fight for what I believed in. It was her gentle and confident nature that had influenced me to do the right thing as I lived my life. All of this information I had received naturally day by day as I was growing up. It was so subtle when I was a child. Now, as an adult—an adult preparing to say goodbye—all those precious daily lessons came sharply into focus.

I lay there with my head on her bed, gently touching her hands, drifting in and out of sleep. Any little movement she made jolted me alert and assured me she was all right. Having a 24-hour nurse available within six feet of my mother gave me a different sense of security. When I would wake through the night, I would see them watching her vital signs, and it gave me greater appreciation of doctors and nurses and what they do for us all during these times. Here they were watching through the night to make sure our mother was as comfortable as possible. They were the most comforting hospital people I had ever met in my life.

I dozed back off to sleep, and the next morning was here before I knew it. The rest of the day, family members took their turns to be with Mom alone. Thankfulness was so powerful. I was grateful that we had that opportunity to share with her and that she would hear us before she passed. I was the last to speak with her that day.

When it was my turn, I approached the side of her bed. She was awake, and our eyes connected almost as an embrace. A feeling of pure, unspoken love and respect filled my body, putting aside the load my own thoughts had created. Even if it was only momentary, I was grateful for the reprieve. Just being near her melted my heart. I knew everything was okay. I moved close to her, sitting on the side of her bed so that I could look directly into her eyes.

I told her that I wouldn't let this drag on for days, as I had promised. I explained that I just wanted to see a few more CAT scans before I made any irreversible decisions. I knew what she had wanted should this day come—no life support. I fought back the tears when I told her I loved her. The memory of that conversation almost one year ago flashed into my mind. It had been a good but serious talk about her wishes. At the time it had seemed a natural and loving conversation, some idea so far away in time. She had tried so often to have her desires heard by my brother and sisters. They all had a difficult time reconciling with the idea of her passing. I reassured her that she would have it her way, exactly as she wanted.

I remember I told her that I thought she had done a wonderful job raising me by herself after Dad had passed, a way to move my thoughts from the awareness of the promise I had made. I was so appreciative and privileged to have her as my mother. She was a wonderful person, and I would always love her and remember all she did for us.

I fought so hard to keep my voice from cracking or from collapsing like a small child overcome with fear. I knew she understood my pain, my fear of losing her to the unknown. I stopped talking and just stared into her eyes for the answer I was looking for—something to reassure me that I was going to do the right thing.

I took notice of a shift within her. I felt drawn into her eyes. Time seemed to stop, and we became encapsulated in a single moment. At that very instant, when all seemed hopeless and the weight was beginning to bear down once more, she lifted her left hand slowly up to my face. The movement took me completely by surprise, for she had remained nearly still since the injury. She was very weak and her right side was paralyzed, so this took a great deal of effort for her.

Seeing this jolted me. It was clear that something profound was occurring. Even her nurse took notice of her efforts. The soft touch of her fingers on my face and the expression in her eyes shattered me into a million pieces. Without a word, she relayed complete conversations with such tenderness and love. Through that touch, more clearly than ever she offered her thanks and support for the strength she knew it would take for me to make the decision to remove life support. She ran her hand down the side of my face as though instantly binding the pieces of me back together. Her hand came to rest on my chin for what felt like an eternity.

I found her love complete and solid, comforting as a truth that would not be denied. I could not bear the thought of not having her on the earth. I had every good intention of comforting her, and she was using her last bit of strength to support me, which I loved, but it made me feel guilty all the more. I managed to keep eye contact with her, although I honestly don't know how I did it. She knew she could depend on me to be strong for her. She thanked me for doing the right thing for her through that touch.

But how would I manage? Was I hallucinating? This was the last thing I really wanted to hear. I knew what this meant for her, and I was horrified at the thought.

She was still holding on to my chin when suddenly the silver chain I was wearing came away from the confines of my shirt, exposing her wedding ring. I watched her eyes lower and become transfixed on the ring. It was easy to imagine what she was thinking. I quickly explained to her that the doctors had said that her fingers would swell because of the stroke, so the nurse had given me the ring for safekeeping so they wouldn't have to cut it off. I feebly tried to rationalize that when the swelling went down, I would put her wedding ring back on for her.

Her hand slid from my chin to grasp her ring. I told her that if she let go of the ring, I'd try to put it back on her finger right away. She released her grip calmly and lowered her hand to the side of her body, all the while watching me intently as I slid the ring easily on her finger. I smiled. I told her that we would stay with her and suggested that she try and get some rest.

I didn't want to leave her, but I knew she needed a break. We had been in and out of her room all day. I gently persuaded her to get some rest and sat silently by her bedside until she was in a deep sleep. I walked through the doorway into the hall of the hospital feeling solemn and confused. This was all completely overwhelming. Was I really prepared for this? How could I possibly summon the needed courage?

Chapter Four

Recognizing Passion

When I wasn't with my mother, I was often in the waiting room with my family. We spent much time reminiscing about our life on the farm. It seemed a comforting and healing pastime.

My father could have only been described as a determined and dependable man. He stood six foot four, with rich dark hair and bright blue eyes, his frame over two hundred pounds and well-muscled from working every day on the family farm. A quiet man unless he needed to communicate something, he tended to the crops and cattle from sunup to sundown, instilling by example a hard-driving work ethic in his brood.

Mom likewise never seemed to stop moving. She cleaned, washed clothes, mended, sewed, tended a huge garden, and cooked for the family. She managed to cook breakfast, make all of our lunches and put up a large supper each evening without fail. Although she would have loved an immaculate house, I'm sure, she made do with a clean one. Still, with so many of us, the challenge of keeping our small farmhouse tidy was never-ending. But she managed without a complaint. She was resilient, filled with love and concern and always quick with encouragement.

Both my parents maintained strong faith and passed the values and principles they believed to their offspring. However, while Mom enjoyed attending church and worshiping with others, including her children, Dad preferred his quiet soulful time alone with God in his black leather chair, reading from his Bible.

We were raised to handle challenges and solve problems, and thank God. I was going to need every ounce of that knowledge to get through this situation.

An occurrence during one springtime calving season in many ways exemplified our lives on the farm. I was eight years old and it was a bitter cold night. Because Dad was already overburdened with work, it fell to the children to take on two-hour shifts all through the night to check on the pregnant cows. Calving season lasted from March to May, and unfortunately, winter's chill often remained well into spring. It was our job to know if a calf had been born in the middle of the night during freezing temperatures. Usually this didn't happen. However, the last thing we could afford was to have a newborn calf freeze to death, so there were to be no chances taken.

One of my sisters and I were making our rounds. We noticed a newborn calf lying on the hard-packed snow out in the corral. I remember it vividly. My own nose nearly frozen, I couldn't imagine how cold that little calf lying on the snow and ice must have been. My sister and I looked at each other, and we knew we dare not wake our dad to ask for help. Yet we couldn't leave the calf exposed in such conditions. There was no way it would have survived out there.

It so happened I was paired on this particular night shift with my one sister who hated cows. As we began in earnest to assess the situation and discuss some possible solutions to this dilemma, the cows began milling closer and closer. This unnerved my sister, who rashly jumped into one of the feed troughs for safety while she screamed and shouted orders at me.

The new calf weighed at least as much as I did. Annoyed at her behavior but also freezing, I refrained from commenting on her unconventional method of helping. Not wanting to miss any more sleep than necessary, I picked up the calf. My adrenaline had taken over, and I carefully stomped my way towards the barn, closely followed by the mother cow, her hot and angry breath steaming on the back of my neck.

I laugh now thinking about my sister perched safely inside the feed trough. All she could see in the moonlight was a big brown mass, legs dangling every-where, and a raging mama cow in hot pursuit of me carrying her baby away. I was actually surprised she didn't wake up half the county with her screaming and carrying on—my sister, not the cow. Finally, she yelled her last threat at me, leapt out of the trough and bolt-ed through the snow ahead of me, headed to the barn. At last making herself useful, she threw open the barn doors, and I made my way back to a warm stall closely followed by the mother cow. I laid the bleating calf in piled straw where it could be with its mother in a safe, dry space. My sister and I stood there amazed at the entire experience and found ourselves just watching the two settle into their new home. They were going to be all right, and even looked grateful as we left. We fought the snow drift back to the house in exhausted mutual silence.

From a young age it has been my nature to jump in and take care of things. I could have been seriously hurt in that case; mama cows aren't docile and kind when it comes to protecting their young. The sheer weight alone of carrying the baby while it squirmed, trying to get back to its mother, and the fact that I could have been badly kicked—all that aside, I had done it. My father was both amazed and stunned that I had managed that on my own at my age.

I looked around the waiting room at my brother and sisters. They were exhausted, and their bleak expressions reminded me of the Dakota winter promising frigid temperatures. There was nothing to be done; it came every year, and we tried to be as cheerful as possible. When the first snow fell, we'd hurry through our chores to feel the exhilaration of racing old car hoods down a nearby snow-covered hill. Our hoods would dash over rocks, jumping and leaping through the air, often tossing us aside; we laughed and raced back up the hill, relentless for another jaunt. This along with the snowball fights, creating snowmen and snow angels provided hours of winter fun. There was never a doubt about having a white Christmas. We did learn to make the best out of trying times. But there was one winter that stopped us in our tracks.

It was Christmas of 1975 when our mother, the very pillar of strength and embodiment of energy, whispered that she didn't feel well and retired early. In fact, completely out of character, she had complained about a headache and ended up lying down for most of that day. This was so unlike her we all fell quiet.

The local hospital diagnosed her with encephalitis and meningitis. Before I knew it she was admitted to the larger Fargo hospital eight hours away. Each trip there meant a disheartening feeling as I watched her lying there silent, lost in a deep state of unconsciousness for the next six and a half months.

One day in particular I sat in the corner of the room and looked at my mother lying still in the bed, and I wondered when there would be a change. I suppose to some it may have looked as though I was exhausted, or so sad at the circumstances that I wasn't capable of hearing or understanding. Perhaps that's why the doctor and the priest took such liberties when they came in to discuss my mom's prognosis with my father. I was eleven years old—I will never forget it. They came in quietly and addressed my father not more than four feet away from me, completely clear and audible. I was horrified when I heard the words, "We don't expect her to live through the night."

We don't expect her to live through the night? It just couldn't be happening. I know they spoke a while longer, but honestly, I'm uncertain of anything else that was said after that. A thin stream of pain had begun to spread quickly through every vein in my body, and with it, a sadness so deep it seemed indescribable.

They appeared unaware or unconcerned that I sat there listening to every word. As I looked at my mother and saw that she was bluish in color, the searing pain in my heart seemed impossible to bear, and the thought of losing my mom forever took my breath away. My emotions of fear, anger and deep sorrow combined, causing nothing but confusion.

I couldn't understand why they couldn't fix her—why I couldn't fix her. Why did she have to die? I slid out of the room quietly, my feet taking me aimlessly through the hospital floors. I came across a room in a dazed stupor—the chapel—and disappeared through the doors. The chapel, though small, was comfortable and quiet. I sat still for a moment, took a deep breath, and became aware of a presence. I was not alone. It was a warm, tender sensation. A wave of comfort flooded through me and numbed the awareness of any pain. There was a distinct feeling of love at such a deep level that it enveloped me and completely relaxed and gave way, melting me into the pew.

I instantly, naturally, began praying as I had grown accustomed to doing, though I felt more confident and secure than I ever had before. I didn't care about who or what God was. All I knew was that He was the only one who could possibly make my mother well again. I sat for hours pleading for divine intervention. I begged Him to let my mom stay with us.

I remembered my mom had spoken of her faith, but at that time I was too young, and my mind primarily was filled with the abundance of the physical world and the wonder of nature. Now, however, I was full of questions, and frustration was building as the answers didn't seem to be coming.

I was scared and confused, but somehow I took every last bit of my own energy and directed it into prayer for my mom. I couldn't imagine my life without her. Unaware that time was passing quickly, I stayed up all night in the chapel. The walls of my mom's room began to glow with the dawn's light as I entered after my evening in His presence. Even though I was exhausted, I felt peaceful. I had done all I knew to do.

The doctor visited soon after, completely ignoring my existence once more. He muttered to himself, something about it being a miracle that my mother had come through the night. Again, I sat in the chair in her room while my father and the doctor talked.

From that day forward things felt different, and they were better for my mother. It was two and a half weeks later when the word came that Mom had fully emerged from her sleep. The coma had passed. I was relieved and thankful. I had been heard that night praying for a miracle in the chapel. I was jubilant. I knew one thing for certain: it was real, that connection and peace I had felt that night in the chapel.

I didn't make another trip to Fargo. I was told that my mother was improving and was being moved to a hospital in Grand Forks to begin her physical therapy closer to home. It was after she woke that the doctors discovered she had suffered a stroke, for she had been left paralyzed on her left side. From that day forward her smile was always a little crooked, but still a joy to see. Her smile bothered her for years to come. To me, it was special. It represented the mark of a miracle. Every time I saw her smile, it reminded me that she had stayed with us. God had been merciful and let me keep my mother.

My father mentioned that the doctors wanted to put Mom in a nursing home, something he was adamantly against. They felt that she would need assistance for the rest of her life, and with the farm it might prove too much to keep her safely at home. My father would not hear of it. He had not left my mother's side for the past seven months, and he had no intention of packing it in and losing her now that she was awake.

I knew my mother and father shared a special bond. They didn't say much, but the way they looked at each other even in passing was unearthly. It was a deep, mutual glance that seemed to reach soul to soul. They loved and respected each other, and they could trust each other. I didn't think much of it at the time, except that it was just a given that moms and dads were supposed to love each other like they were supposed to love us. Dad's unyielding vigil over Mom while she was in the hospital gave me a whole new perspective on just how deep their love was for one another. He was there day in and day out. Presumptuously, I had always thought my father cared most for the farm, our livelihood. A foolish boy has grown up since those days.

Father had informed those of us still living at home that Mom was coming back and that he would need us to continue her physical therapy if she were to recover and gain more control over her body. This was our new job. I considered our home physical therapy duties a blessing. We spent countless hours helping Mom get strong enough to walk, dress herself and eventually drive. After almost losing her, I relished the time spent with her. I would wheel her up to a large wall we had in our kitchen and proceed to help her by standing her up, placing her hands flat against the wall for balance. Her quiet determination was nothing short of inspirational.

"Take one hand off the wall, Mom," I would coax her.

Eventually she not only could stand on her own, but could walk and perform all her normal motherly duties. I was so thankful for the time I had with my mom that summer of 1976 as I turned twelve. Seven months is a long time to let your muscles atrophy, so it took a long while before Mom completely got her strength back, but she never complained or stopped trying.

I had crawled on the bus the first day of the new school year and a voice rang through the air, making fun of the ad we had placed in the local paper requesting donations to help with the medical expenses. I was horrified and took such a blow to my self-confidence. I couldn't fathom how anyone, regardless of age, could be so cruel and couldn't feel compassion for another family's suffering. Regardless, my mom was home and we were all together once more. We were, however, a hundred thousand dollars in debt at the time due to hospital bills—and that was with insurance.

A year later, as I was getting off the bus I saw several semi trucks parked down by the feedlots loading up the cattle. I rushed into the house, breathless and worried; I knew we didn't sell the cattle until spring. I raced to my father. He just sat there in his black leather chair, staring straight ahead, completely still. I asked him what was going on.

Maybe he answered; I couldn't tell you. I was feeling my blood draining from my head, numbed by the lack of expression in his voice, the sadness on his face, and his lifeless appearance as he sank into his leather chair. I made my way out to the feedlots, looking for answers. All of the cattle were being loaded up into the truck, even one my dad had given me. I cried when I watched my red cow walk up the ramp and get loaded into the semi. They left a few horses, including the one I had received for my seventh birthday. However, no one would give me the reason why this was happening.

It's amazing how fast news travels in a small town. The next day on the school bus, everyone was buzzing with questions. I had nothing to share. I came home every day to find my dad in his leather chair as though he had never moved. The man that I knew to be a constant source of strength, continuously working, sat stationary.

Completely baffled, I would go in to him and say hello and ask him how he was doing. He would always respond, flatly, "Fine." He would try to engage and ask me how my day was. But he had sunken emotionally, barely making eye contact. My sisters were lost in their high school experiences, and I was left to my own world, which had suddenly become very quiet and lonely.

This was a man so foreign from the man I had come to admire and love over the years of my life. He sat in that chair, yet was as vacant as though it was only his ghost. Every day I wished to come home to find my father's hopeless phase over, and my dad up and working, smiling again. After the cattle were gone, his world became more and more dim and quiet. No one would talk about it, and the lack of acknowledgement was driving me crazy. I longed for the answers, but there just didn't seem to be any. Mom went about her work as though nothing had happened, as though nothing had changed. She continued to mend and sew to make extra money. I turned to God again. I asked him to fix my father as He had answered my prayers with my mother.

Chapter Five

Love, Mutual Respect
and Commitment

I wrestled with everything that was happening. How could we have all come through such a challenge with our mom, only to have our father falling ill? He was nearly catatonic and slipping rapidly away from his family. Why wasn't God making him better? In just two years' time everything had changed so drastically. I longed for the direction my father had offered in the past, the way he expected his family to rally and get the job done, the way I had worked for his approval.

One day in January I came home from school and went in to see my father as usual, only to find his chair empty. Mom explained that Dad wasn't feeling well and had gone to the hospital. It had been almost two years to the day since my mom had been admitted to the hospital. A feeling of dread loomed in the air.

We visited him as often as we could, and he acted the same as when he was home in his chair. He just lay there, distant, without a fight left in him. He would soon turn fifty four, and it looked as though we would be ushering in his new year in the hospital. My sister Donna and I made him a birthday sign to take to his room. He seemed so lifeless and detached.

It was eight days later while I was in school that someone knocked on the classroom door, and my teacher disappeared around the small corner of the hallway to answer. She soon returned and motioned for me. There was a crushing weight on my chest as I gathered my things and made my way to the door to find one of my older sisters waiting for me. Her eyes expressed mourning, and I dared not ask. We walked down the school's concrete steps together, and she told me that our father had passed away. The air was knocked out of me. He was gone.

We drove along in silence, my sister, her husband and I. As we approached the farmhouse, I could see the cars of neighbors who had brought condolence meals. I found myself sitting again in a room watching the world go by. People moved and spoke. There was speculation that he had died of lung cancer since he had smoked. I chose to believe that for years, suppressing the memory of his vacant expression—not a symptom of lung cancer to my knowledge.

Perhaps my mother and family felt I needed protection. Or perhaps they were just as confused and wounded as I was and found the best way to deal with uncomfortable events was to put the nose to the grindstone and make their way through it. Whatever the reason, no one said anything to me about my father.

I felt alone once more, until the signs of anger began to seep out from around my edges. I felt determined to get answers, but it was to no avail, which angered me even further. I was angry at God. There was an answer, of course. But the language of God is mystical and rarely understood when approached with hostility—an approach seemingly out of reach for me. I just didn't understand. I didn't know how to pick up the pieces. I was lost and couldn't get my bearings. How could I survive constantly feeling like I was losing ground in a landslide? Everything was different now. The cattle were gone, my father was gone. It was quiet and I felt alone.

I was in a haze at the funeral, seated in front of my father's open casket. I couldn't tell you what was said on my father's behalf, or the specific messages at the sermon of what I imagine were reminders for us of God's infinite glory and my father's newfound peace. Sitting in that pew felt familiar and reminded me of when I had prayed all night for my mother in Fargo.

The air became thin and cool and I struggled to stay present, but found myself carried back through time, lost in memories.

"Come with me, son." We walked out of the house and onto the front porch, Dad and I. "Have a look in the barn, Tom."

I was flying that day, light on my feet as I ran to the barn. I opened the door with excitement to see a mare and newborn foal. The foal was mine, my seventh birthday present. I named him Champ. I couldn't contain myself or my gratitude. I ran back to share my enthusiasm with my dad. He glowed that day, as I remembered. He loved that we shared a respect and love for horses.

I could watch that little foal run around the pasture with its mother for hours. He became a strong yearling, and when he turned two my father made sure he was at a gentleman's ranch that started young horses. At the end of a month he was ready to come home. I saw my father's face. Everything in his eyes told me that he believed in me, that I could ride my horse. Even to this day the confidence he instilled in me is as clear as day; it was truth. I could trust it, and horses—horses were honest creatures. They never hid their feelings.

We drove to where my horse was being trained, and when we got there I leapt out of the truck and ran to Champ, now a beautiful, big gelding. Before I knew it I was being tossed onto his back, my father's strong arms lifting me. I rode him bareback all eight miles home. My father drove the old green truck alongside of us. I rode in the ditches looking over toward the truck, my father's slight smile of pride easily seen. People passing in their cars would wave as they went by. My mother's face as we trotted up the driveway was beautiful, one of such relief, pure happiness that I had returned in one piece. As Champ and I headed back to the barn I felt so connected, so happy. I honestly thought I was going to burst. I couldn't believe my good fortune.

I just knew that I would always have horses in my life. As I turned Champ out to run and get reacquainted with the other horses, I felt a sense of internal encouragement. This really was a big accomplishment for me. I watched Champ romp and felt so much admiration at having the trust of such a powerful animal. He was so kind to me. To add to my further delight, my father had trusted me enough to ride a green horse at the age of nine. I was on top of the world.

As I left the happy dream, I noticed my mother's face was quite different today, somber and long. I caught my breath. The frustration and struggles over the years came flooding back, and I was back at the funeral with the rest of my family. My brother and sisters sat quietly in their own thoughts, trying to make sense of the turn of events. Our parents had always tried to teach us the importance of integrity and our word. They had taught us that we could trust them. Dad had taught me lifelong values of work, responsibility and the love and care for our animals, especially the horses.

I only glanced at him briefly, and my mind carried me back to a conversation we had had when my mother was in the hospital. I had just come back in from my visit to the chapel. He told me that he too had prayed all night. He had prayed to spare my mother, and that he would gladly go in her place. It was all coming back to me. Where did he go? Was his prayer heard and accepted? Did he sacrifice himself for my mom? Was he putting me on notice that morning he'd confided in me?

I was back to square one, now angry at God for apparently listening to my father. But if that were true, then he had sacrificed himself for her. I loved him even more for his prayer, and the grief all but overtook me. Didn't God know how much his wife and children needed him? Everything I thought I was beginning to figure out had tied me into knots, an indiscernible mess.

I waited until the line of grieving people had paid their last respects to ask Mom if I could have a bit of time alone with my father. She was more than hesitant, but she acceded to my persistence. Slowly I made my way to the large wooden casket. I could feel only the edges of sadness within me. I could see his body, resting.

I asked him again, "Why? Why did you say that to God? How could God need you more than we do? I promise, Dad, I'll be the best son I can be. I promise I'll take care of Mom."

I had no idea how I was going to fulfill that promise, but I had a feeling I would manage. I mustered up all my courage to lean over and kiss him on his forehead. The coolness of his skin on my lips shocked me. His body was cold to the touch, and a chill ran through me likewise. He wasn't there. My father was dead. In an abrupt flash I was overcome with fear. The realization of how fragile life is, one's mortality, and the permanence of death began to overtake my consciousness.

I ran to the bathroom and locked myself in a stall. Now thirteen, I found myself afraid of death. I didn't understand what death was or what it meant, or how it came. I began to cry hysterically. My mom had asked several of my uncles to find me and they were knocking on the door, trying to coax me out.

"Tommy, we need to go. Please come out. Your mom is worried about you. Everyone is leaving to take your dad to the cemetery."

I did come out, finally, and got into the car that was on its way to the cemetery. I stared out the window, hoping the drive would take forever. The cars drove in procession into the cemetery with my dad's remains. My mind once again became cluttered with questions and concerns. Where was he, exactly? Did he show up to his own funeral? Did he hear my promise? Could he feel how much we loved him?

I stood next to my mom at the cemetery. There were so many people there. I felt lost and detached. The priest spoke, and I found myself soothed by the gentle pace and tone of his voice. However, I could not tell you what his words expressed. People made comments that were beautiful, I'm sure, but I couldn't tell you what was said. I didn't want to leave the cemetery as my mother gently guided me into the car. I crawled into the back seat so I could turn around and send a message to my dad that I loved him as we drove away.

Chapter Six

What in Heaven's Name?

By the time we returned to the farm, all of my sisters and my brother and their families had filled the house. I gave up my room and slept in the living room on the couch. Midway through the night I woke, paralyzed with fear. Moonlight had crept through the window curtains, laying shadows across the many funeral flower bouquets around the room. I felt alone and scared.

We kept busy getting Mom healthy again. My sisters and I enjoyed the time with her. I had noticed my father's subtle exhaustion, his withdrawal, but had tried to ignore it, hoping that one day he would bounce back to the father I remembered. It never occurred to me that he wouldn't survive. I think that shocked me the most. And that it had happened so quickly. I kept busy so as to ignore the memory of his chilled skin, not wanting to face the idea of death.

As I mentioned, my parents held mutual values and convictions, and these were instilled in me by different means. I remember in particular a defining moment. My father had bought me my first saddle. We didn't own a saddle after we had Champ broke to ride by a professional, so that first year I learned to ride him bareback. Dad had saved money for quite a while so he could present me with the saddle for my tenth birthday. It was crafted from rich black leather and had simple tooling. I loved to take deep breaths, my nose nearly touching the seat as I inhaled the clean, fresh smell of the new leather. I ran to the barn to get my horse and brought him up to the front pasture to saddle him in front of my parents, who gazed lovingly at their son through the large picture window. The saddle secured and cinched to Champ's back, I was finally ready to ride in a saddle. I climbed the wood rail fence and lowered myself gently onto the saddle.

I was taken completely by surprise when without warning, Champ jumped into the air, bucking violently. Before I knew it, I was sailing through the air and landed with a thud on the dirt. My parents ran outside, having seen my rodeo ride, and came to me. I lay dazed and motionless, so they could only fear the worst. Fortunately, I had only had the wind knocked from me and was lying there trying to regain my strength. Unfortunately, this process of being thrown saw a number of repeats.

Dad and I sat together for a few moments in silence while I gathered my composure. After a long pause, we discussed what was happening. It was my dad who made the explanation easy. Horses appreciate our kindness, but they are still prey animals, and their first instinct is not emotional but reactionary. Champ was reacting to something that simply didn't feel right to him. I suppose in some ways we all do that. He felt threatened and restricted; bucking and running was how he was wired to survive. After a few more minutes thinking about my dad's words, I realized that my horse hadn't felt the tightness of a cinch around his belly in over a year, not since he had been originally broke to ride.

Filling the empty void and blocking the grief that my father's death had created could only be done with constant physical momentum. I didn't have my father to follow behind me to make sure everything was done right. It was all on me. Regardless, as I worked I sometimes found myself contemplating thoughts of where he must be, about where he had gone after he left us. He had been gone for nearly two years now. I could still hear his driving voice as clear as day, lecturing my brother, sisters and me about taking pride in our work and doing it right the first time. As usual, I wasn't about to let my father down—not then, not now.

I naturally looked for activities that felt familiar and reminded me of him. I decided to show a steer. This was also this first time that I had handled any kind of cow since he'd let everything go right before he got sick. When I worked with the little steer, it reminded me of how hard my dad had labored to take care of our cattle and to keep them healthy and safe.

It was the day of the fair, and I headed to the barn. I was filled with anticipation and excitement. I immediately went to work bathing the steer. Finally satisfied that all dirt had been removed, I left him tied up to a post to stand in the sun to dry. I had worked up quite an appetite after hours of grooming and manicuring, so I took off to the house for lunch, leaving him dozing in the sunshine, his sleepy eyes half shut.

Re-energized from one of Mom's hearty lunches, I headed back to the corral where I had left the steer. Just as I rounded the corner of the barn, sheer panic set in. He was gone. I stood in disbelief. The gentleman who had agreed to take my prize steer to the fair was coming that very afternoon.

I scanned the horizon. Cows are herd animals and never seem to feel completely comfortable without others of their kind surrounding them. We had leased the property out to a cattle farmer who currently had a herd somewhere on the thousand acres. I racked my brain, trying to remember the last time I had seen the herd. The answer came to me: a couple of miles away on the northeast corner.

I took off running over hills and through pastures, desperate to catch up with my steer. Gasping for breath, not thinking twice about the thick and heavy heat, I crested a low rise in the rock-laden, sparse pasture, and I spotted the herd. Sure enough, there was my little steer running around like crazy.

Watching him was nothing short of enchanting. My steer had been kept away from his buddies the past several months so I could keep him sedentary in the barn, feeding him rich grains and hay, intending to fatten him up for his day at the fair. He looked so carefree and simply beside himself with joy. He trotted back and forth, never settling down. The problem was, pounds were melting off his body. All that time I had kept him separated, trying to control his fate and nature, only to have those efforts reduced in a few moments.

I quietly slid through the grasses so as not to spook the herd. If the lead cow got startled and fled for any reason, the whole group would follow, along with my little steer. There was always one dominant cow that led the heard. When I had worked the cows with my father it was always a challenge to move the herd from one pasture to another, keeping the lead cow happily going in the direction we preferred.

As I got closer I could see that my show steer was dripping foamy wet from the two-mile run and his frolicking. Carefully I made my way to the lead rope still attached to his halter, and with one quick move I leapt for the end of the rope. I was exhausted at this point, and if he had decided to run again I don't think I had it in me to try and hold back his 700-pound body. Thank heaven he was as tired as I was.

After this little adventure, it looked as though he had lost at least half his body weight. I was crushed. This was my first show steer, and I had worked so hard to make him as perfect as possible. I had worked tirelessly on his appearance and made sure through hours of practice that he would stand still for a judge.

The preparation and effort were rewarded in the end. We both arrived at the fair in one piece. I prayed that I would have a well-behaved steer and not an anxious beast on my hands the next day at judging time. To my delight I was placed in the second place group, a true honor since the first place handlers were all veterans with many years of experience in showing steers. Sometimes we think the worst, and it all really does turn out okay—sometimes better than we ever thought it would.

Chapter Seven

Acceptance

Grief is an elusive event. It comes and goes like a tide with no set time. There were times between the two years of my mother's illness and my father's death that I felt fine, busy with the day-to-day events of a young person. Still, there seemed to be this undercurrent of confusion I couldn't put into words. I was not taught about the feelings of grief, that they ebb and flow in and out of stages, sometimes disappearing altogether and then cropping back up when we least expect it. Honestly, I struggled a great deal with the thoughts of death and loss. I don't think I ever got over my father's death; I only became accustomed to living without him. Just when I thought the pain from losing my father had been buried deep inside my soul, something would trigger the memories. I found myself praying for peace, for death to leave me alone.

Now I wonder if I wasn't involved with something more profound at the time, yet was in so much pain I didn't recognize it, a crisis of faith maybe. I began to ponder the ways of God and concepts like death: what it meant and where we went after we died. I was taught this in Mass, so why all the questions? Still, my thoughts were full of heat and emotion, often directed at God in anger, for the way my father had left seemed so cruel to me. I went back and forth with Him, off and on through the years that followed. Why on God's earth had I been able to sway Him to spare my mom, and been ignored (or so it seemed) when I prayed for my dad? With no obvious response from the higher power, I finally came to the conclusion that it would be better not to think about these subjects and stay focused on my work. At least I had some control over that.

I tried to keep the many fond memories of time with my dad alive despite the memory of his cold and lifeless body. Death remained a frightening proposition. Mortality became a taboo subject which I would avoid at all costs. I denied and suppressed any thought or feeling that could possibly lead to that topic. However, I also noticed that it actually didn't come up very often in conversation. Were people afraid, like me? Did they wonder, like I did, what happens to us when we pass on? Is that why they weren't talking? I could only speculate.

I heard mention over time of people who had had near-death experiences. And although investigation of their journeys might have helped me to glean some glimmer of hope, I was so full of emotions suppressed by my own encounters with death that I was not motivated to read even one of them. I was blinded by my own decrees on how to handle the subject. It wasn't like I was going to escape this fate—nobody "gets out alive," after all.

What kind of a God would send his children here with this kind of torment? Why no answers? I knew He could hear me. I had reached him when I prayed for Mom.

Chapter Eight

Divinely Directed

Every now and again in my mind I would replay the phone call, the panic in my sister's voice…

I gazed at my mother, often in and out of sleep, her rosary resting in her hand. Mom had been suffering with arthritis for the last twenty-eight years, some months being worse than others. Still, she managed to gently roll the familiar beads between her fingers. Saying the rosary at that point was so natural for her.

We often searched for comfort silently with one another. Of course, we had all realized this day would eventually come. Yet there was a heavy sadness, accompanied by sheer exhaustion, that was felt by all. As the night wore on, some of us left for the hotel room across the street. A few of us slept in recliners in the reading room on the ICU floor. I couldn't sleep. I generally found myself pacing the hospital floor outside my mother's room, sitting with my mother for hours, or returning to the waiting area to make sure everyone was okay. This was as close to crisis management as I'd ever come, really. They say in a crisis to take care of the basic needs: food, sleep and little else. If you don't manage these, sooner or later the body will collapse. I did so as best I could manage.

We were all praying for a miracle for Mom. We sat around for hours talking, laughing, crying and preparing ourselves for the days to come. Sleep deprivation was certainly setting in for many, but there was nothing to do but endure. We were all too worried to get anything other than maintenance sleep. We would say our goodnights to one another and filter off in different directions. I stayed in the hospital, wandering around for hours, praying for Mom, trying to get a little sleep and checking in on her throughout the night. We were all very quiet and respectful around Mom when she was resting.

Sunday morning came, and we were all hoping to hear something different after they had taken a fourth scan of Mom's brain. We were not allowed to go with her during the procedure, and it troubled me greatly to think that she might be feeling alone and scared. I wished someone had been allowed to be with her. We waited patiently for the doctors to arrive and share what we hoped would be good news.

The tension in the air had been building. Finally, the doctor arrived and sat down with us. He appeared discouraged as he proceeded to tell us that nothing had changed over the course of four days. His prognosis was the same: nothing would change.

We sat there quiet a moment, and then someone asked if she would ever be able to walk or feed herself again. He explained that the stroke was so bad that our mom was left almost completely paralyzed. She had very little movement in her left hand and could move her neck and shoulders a little. He showed us the CAT scan that had just been taken. He said that if the stroke was like the one she had had back in 1976, she would definitely have a chance. But this stroke was far more severe. There was less than a five percent chance that she would ever recover. He stated that in all his years of practice he had never seen anyone recover from such damage.

There it was. We sat there not knowing what to do or say. I remember at one point before he left, I looked over at the doctor and said to him, "Am I jumping the gun by thinking about removing life support?"

He looked me in the eye and he replied in such a compassionate manner that it caught me by surprise. "If your mom wasn't on life support at this point, she would have already passed. It is only the life support that is keeping her with you."

I'll never forget how that felt when he said those words. They resounded throughout my body.

Another gift then, this time with our mother. I knew at that point what we needed to do as a family. As we sat in silence, the doctor asked if we had any more questions. Many of us shook our heads no. We thanked him for his time. As he walked out and closed the door behind him, an overwhelming flow of emotions poured out from us. We hugged each other and we cried.

We sat there for quite some time discussing Mom's prognosis, and we came to the decision to remove life support. My older brother couldn't bear to be the one to tell the doctor and asked me if I could do it. I asked that the life support be removed around noon the following day. I don't really know why that particular hour was so important. Perhaps this gave everyone time in the morning to grapple with their thoughts and prepare. Or perhaps it was because from the bottom of my heart, I was praying for a miracle. I wanted to give God the extra time, just in case.

Chapter Nine

Decision to Accept

Eventually that day my brain began to race. It felt as though some heaviness had taken up residence on the outskirts of my thoughts and was picketing my decision. The questions began to set in. Had I made the right choice? What if I was wrong? What if God needed more time? I'm sure it sounds ludicrous—as if God would need more time, honestly. But at the time, the fear of making that fatal decision could not be ignored. We had all made the decision together, but for some reason, I felt myself unconsciously pulling away, and I felt alone.

I pondered for hours that night about what was going to happen the following day. I don't remember where I tried to rest. Around 6:30 or 7:00 Monday morning I walked into Mom's room and up to her bed, thinking I wouldn't be able to do this. I couldn't remove life support and watch my mother pass away. But I knew I had to. She had made sure we all heard her wishes should it end like this: "Don't leave me on life support." One couldn't make it more clear than that.

I tried to regain the strength I knew I'd need for the day. I was filled with great apprehension and found I could not look her in the eyes. I couldn't come to terms with her wishes regardless of how hard I wrestled with the obvious. My thoughts caromed. When I finally gathered the courage to look at her, I found her gaze piercing and unyielding—the kind of look that can knock you to the floor.

Without question, I knew that she was aware of what I was feeling. I could read it in her gaze. It didn't take me long to hear her thoughts loud and clear, even though her words couldn't come. With all of the turmoil at that time, I still marveled at how she seemed so present, still Mom through and through even though she was trapped in a body that had left her unable to move or speak. Her silence spoke volumes, and I must admit that I did not want to hear what she was trying to relay. I had such respect for her that it was ultimately impossible to ignore her.

"I thought I could depend on you to do the right thing. You promised me the other day that you wouldn't let this drag on. You told me you could handle this because of how strong you are, and here you're having second thoughts about what you're doing to-day," she appeared to be saying.

I couldn't bear it, and I told Mom I had to leave for just a minute and retreated in utter confusion. There had to be another way to recover.

I feared making the wrong choice, a decision that could not be reversed. It was the outcome that I was rejecting, I realized. But when a crisis comes, it is easy to become lost in the uncertainty. Perhaps a change of atmosphere, some fresh air would help. I needed different surroundings to get my head clear.

I walked over to the hotel room where some of my family members were staying. By the time I got there, the heat had risen within me to the point of a minor combustion, and I entered the room with such hostility I could sense my family's concern. Although they asked, I felt I shouldn't share with them how Mom had looked at me moments earlier. She comprehended that I was having second thoughts about removing life support that day. It was her look of utter disappointment in me that crushed me. No one even knew that I had stayed up almost all night praying to God to take Mom as she slept so we didn't have to go through the process of removing life support. That was an unnecessary burden to lay on them. As bad as that would have sounded to some of them, I kept my feelings to myself.

After calming down a bit, I returned to Mom's room.

My sister Donna was sitting with Mom and holding her hand. Donna and I made eye contact, but we didn't say a word. I began pacing back and forth, ruminating over the lack of options. I found myself at the end of the bed, and I removed the blanket from Mom's feet and calves and began gently massaging them and then looking at them carefully. I had hoped that I was seeing some movement in her legs from the stimulation. Grasping for anything at this point, I asked the nurse if I was seeing some movement because my mom was moving on her own, or was it because of the machine. She replied that it was the machine helping to circulate the blood in her legs and feet so she didn't get blood clots. I'm sure it was clear that I was having second thoughts.

I looked at my mom and thought, Mom? Am I doing the right thing? I need to know for sure! I knew Donna was shocked when I questioned the nurse about Mom's movement, but I couldn't be self-conscious about that now. This was too important. When this was over, I was going to have to live with it for the rest of my life. I noticed Donna's face showed sympathy. They were all looking to me for strength, and to be a sounding board with the doctors. It was a great weight.

Still, I continued grasping for a sign from Mom that we shouldn't remove life support. I had become overwhelmed by the comments made to me over the last five days. Too often a well-intentioned family member would approach and express how grateful they were that I was there, how I was the rock of the family, and they wouldn't know what to do without me.

I had continued on through the past few days trying to ignore, push down or forget what I was really feeling—that I first wished that this wasn't happening at all, and then that there was someone else who could do this for me. But not wanting to add to my already burdened family members' problems, I kept my feelings to myself. I'm sure that's got to be right at the top of the psychological "do not do list" for crisis management.

The impact of this burden was gradual but fierce. Finally it rose to the point of nearly too much to handle. I realized the shift setting in almost immediately after I told the doctor to remove life support. I couldn't shake the feeling that I was killing our mother. This was why I had prayed to God Sunday night for hours on end, pleading for Him to take the burden away. I didn't want to, or see how I could, carry the guilt that was contributing to this decision.

The chaplain came by and visited with all of us for a time that morning, a very nice young lady. When she asked if we would like to go in and say a prayer with Mom, we all agreed. We circled around Mom in her bed, and the chaplain stood behind her headboard. I held tight to the bed, trying my hardest not to collapse into tears. I maneuvered my way to where I could easily talk with Mom. I told her that I loved her. With tears building up inside me, I walked to the window and gazed up at the sky. For the first time since we'd arrived in Rochester, it was a beautiful sunny day. At that moment I knew I had started to surrender. A noticeable change occurred inside me, like something just gave way and released.

The chaplain's voice and words were a salve to open wounds, taking the sting out of the day a bit. She finished and left the room quietly. It was only a short time later that the doctor and nurses entered the room and asked the family to leave while they completed the procedure of removing Mom's life support. We filed out into the hallway and waited, holding hands, crying quietly. I remember thinking that this was happening too quickly. I had the facts: this was the best state she could expect, and she did not want long-term care in a nursing home. And there was also no getting away from the fact that she had made her wishes absolutely clear—no reliance on life support.

When the doctor had finished, we came back into the room. We were all stunned. She looked so peaceful without the tubes. It was as though she had a presence about her, around her, a freedom that was expressed in mere sight. Even the left side of her mouth had regained its shape and was no longer droopy. It was nothing short of miraculous. It was as if she had turned forty years younger in the last thirty minutes. I stood next to her for a moment, numbed by the sight of her. Steadily, though, the realization of what this also meant crept back in. My mother was going to die.

I stayed in her room for a while. She seemed to be stable and resting for now, so I decided to return to the hotel and try to get some rest myself for just a bit. I let my brother and sisters know and asked them to call or come get me only if it was an emergency. I'd had little sleep over the past five days, and the deprivation, along with all the pain, was taking its toll.

Chapter Ten

Love Is the Heart of the Matter

I really didn't want to leave my mom, but I knew I would be beyond service to anyone if I did not get some sleep soon. I lay on the bed, and despite all that was happening, the moment was blissful. My eyes quickly closed.

In a matter of minutes the phone rang. Mom was having a hard time breathing, and the nurse wanted to insert a breathing tube. There was confusion and fear in my sister's voice. She did not want anything to be done that went against Mom's wishes. I reassured her that the breathing tube was not life support, only a means of keeping an airway open. I asked her to let the nurse handle this. The papers had been signed, and the hospital wouldn't do anything to go against Mom's wishes. I repeated that the decisions had been made. I could have been more kind with my sister, but I was simply too tired.

Nonetheless, with my desire for sleep thwarted, I returned quickly to Mom's room. The closer I got to the hospital, the more upset I got. With only ten minutes of sleep, I entered Mom's room very upset. The chaos I felt as I entered was more than I could handle. I had spent much of my life questioning the greatest journey called death, but there are journeys for which we cannot fully prepare, neither as one setting out for that farther shore nor as one witnessing another's drifting away. I became short tempered with nearly everyone, except Mom.

I then turned around and looked at the nurse, and I asked her what she was going to do for Mom. She quickly explained that she had phoned a respiratory therapist to get an appropriate size of breathing tube. This nurse had been in the room earlier to assist the doctor while removing Mom's life support. She had noticed irritation in Mom's throat when she removed the breathing tube earlier. She only wanted advice from a specialist so she wouldn't hurt our mother unnecessarily. She advised all of us to leave the room while she inserted the tube.

I couldn't handle all the pressure that I was feeling from my family. About twenty minutes had gone by when I got up and walked out of the hospital, feeling exhausted and overwhelmed with the day. I walked right past a few of my siblings on the way out of the hospital without a word or even an acknowledgement.

I got myself outside and phoned my friend Mary in California. I needed someone to talk to. She was a close friend, and I longed for some comfort. We only spoke on the phone briefly, and she stressed the importance of rest in emotional times such as this. She felt I was overly tired and needed to step away from the hospital for more than a few minutes and get some serious rest. I knew she was right. She impressed further that if I had accepted the role of family spokesman, of course my family was going to look to me in our time of crisis. I understood what she said, but was too fatigued to really comprehend the depth of what she was trying to tell me. I hung up with her insisting that I go get some rest.

I was walking across the grass lawn between the hospital and the hotel when I spotted a couple of my sisters and my niece walking back toward the hospital. I called to them a few times before they heard me. They came to me and I let them know that I was so exhausted—I felt completely taxed both physically and emotionally and just needed rest. In fact, my legs were weak, so weak I needed to sit on the lawn. I didn't lower myself gracefully, but rather my legs gave way and collapsed to a sitting position on the lawn.

The lightheadedness and weakness were almost overwhelming, yet still I struggled to stand up and continue to the hotel. With my sisters on either side helping me, I didn't make it twenty feet when my body completely gave out and I fell to one side. My sisters reacted quickly to prevent my crashing to the ground. My arms around their shoulders now, we proceeded slowly across the street to the hotel lobby.

We had almost made it halfway through the crosswalk when my legs gave out from under me. I was unable to walk, and my sisters literally dragged me the rest of the way across the street, into the lobby and directly to the elevator door as though I were an awkward piece of furniture. Once at the elevator door, I braced myself a little with my hands on the wall, saying I was okay. The elevator door opened and I tried to step forward but immediately collapsed to the ground inside the elevator.

A couple of nurses eating in the hotel diner saw what had happened and ran over to see if they could assist. One of them took my pulse, reported it was very rapid, and suggested I get to the emergency room just next door. I only remember hearing the words "emergency room" and pronouncing that I did not want to go to the hospital. I wasn't thinking clearly, that's true. But feelings had taken over logic, and I didn't want to risk taking family away from Mom in her last hours.

I didn't want my mother to feel my presence in the emergency room.

I tried to move my legs and was unsuccessful, so I asked one of my sisters to get the wheelchair I had spotted at the entrance of the hotel. After she had gotten the wheelchair, I managed to pull myself up into it. I asked my sisters to put my legs onto the foot rests. They commented that my legs were like cement hardened to the floor.

They finally were successful with getting my legs onto the foot rests, but with much effort. I had no control over or feeling in my legs. I didn't understand what was happening to me. I tried to steady my mind and think. I knew I was completely exhausted from the events of the last five days, but not being able to move my legs made absolutely no sense whatsoever.

I sat in the wheelchair, thinking if I could just sit for a few moments I would regain the feeling in my legs. However, the longer I sat there, the worse I felt. The room began to spin, and I became weaker and weaker. My legs were paralyzed, and I was now experiencing excruciating pain in my abdomen. When I began to black out, I asked my sister to call 911. A few minutes later paramedics arrived from the hospital.

The paramedics started asking me supposedly easy questions—things I should know, like my name, where I was and so on. It took two big paramedics and a police officer to move me out of the wheelchair and onto the gurney. I looked up at one of them standing behind me and said, "It's a good thing I lost thirty pounds last year, isn't it?" They snickered. It was obvious they were in a quandary about the heaviness of my body. It didn't make any sense to them either.

I was finally on the gurney and safely in the ambulance, and we raced the 100 feet across the street and to the emergency room. Once I'd been admitted, a nurse came into my room and questioned me about what had happened and my symptoms. I tried to make some kind of sense as I explained, and she immediately got on the phone to the doctor. The emergency room was bustling with patients that evening. The nurse urged me to be patient. I had every intention of getting up and leaving whenever the feeling in my legs came back and said so to the nurse. She advised me not to.

About twenty minutes later the spell had passed. I could feel my legs again. I got dressed and carefully made my way out to the waiting area where my sisters were waiting. We made our way back to the hotel across the street, and I checked myself into a room. I was convinced that if I could just sleep, things would be very different. I lay on the bed and for the first time in days felt relieved. Perhaps my energy level was depleted from my trying to support everyone else. Yes, that made sense. My pseudo paralysis was my own body telling me to take care of myself.

One of my sisters stayed behind to keep an eye on me. I mentioned to her that my legs were starting to get numb again, and she massaged them, trying to improve circulation. There was an air of concern rising. Something profound was happening. I knew it; I just couldn't put my finger on it. I was stronger and healthier than I had ever been, so not even exhaustion could explain this. I was feeling nervous again. I had thought I was out of the woods. I didn't understand what was happening to me. I could not move again. I was in the best shape of my life. Why was this happening?

Most of my family was with our mother, and everyone was settling in for a long night ahead. I was very relieved to have someone stay with me that night. I was flat out scared about what was going on. A controlled panic set in. I knew that if I tried to get up or even move, I couldn't. The paralysis had come back, and once again I was completely unable to move from my waist down.

My arms crossed over my chest had become very heavy, the weight of them alone pushing the air out of me. I asked my sister to please move my arms because I was having a hard time breathing. When she picked them up to lay them at my side, I was only aware of the pressure of her lifting them, as if she had moved dead weight. I had lost the feeling in my arms as well. I tried desperately over and over to move them, but I just couldn't.

I tried to keep my composure and remain calm, telling myself that it was all in my mind. I tried to distract myself by focusing on eliminating the anxiety first; then I'd work on moving. I lay there quietly praying for this to stop. Nothing was changing. The insight brought a terror. All I could do was move my head at this point.

I had needed to go to the bathroom when I came into the room earlier. I had only planned to lie down for a minute. I asked my sister to call our brother so he could carry me into the restroom. My panic had risen, not helped by the humiliation of my brother having to clean up after me. My head was spinning. Thoughts raced by so fast I couldn't collect them.

With astounding force came a loud rushing sound, a great current of energy that felt like a gale. I felt Mom rush into my body through the top of my head. Lying there completely hostage, I could hear her say to me very loud and clear, "Now how does that feel?

I'm lying up here completely paralyzed with only a small amount of movement in my left hand, messing myself, having strangers clean me up, and you have been feeling guilty about taking me off life support? You know this is not how I want to live. Release all guilt for what you have done… NOW."

There had been a tremendous amount of suppressed feeling for days, yet with those words arrived a sense of release that was overwhelming. I knew at that moment why I was experiencing the paralysis and the weakness, the panic and loss of control. I needed to feel what she was experiencing to get it.

Suddenly I was free. At the utterance of her last word, the guilt that I had been carrying around since I had told the doctors to remove life support was gone. I felt as light as a feather—although I still couldn't move. I finally understood. I was experiencing paralysis as a result of feeling guilty. But if that was it, why wasn't the feeling coming back now that I realized what was going on?

Regardless, I asked my sister to phone everyone and have them come over to the hotel. The word spread quickly, and soon the room was filled with my brother and sisters. I related to them what was happening and what Mom had managed to tell me. They listened, and I felt most of them did so without prejudging, even when I reported that our mother had entered my body through the top of my head. However, because I had managed to hide my feelings of guilt for the most part, they didn't fully understand why I should be stricken this way. I tried to explain how difficult it was for me to be the one to actually tell the doctor our decision to stop life support.

The part of my mind that jumps to the worst case scenario had convinced me that when I returned to California, my brother and sisters would change their minds about what we should have done for Mom and blame me. I had tried to fight off those thoughts and push them out of my head, but I would lose every battle. Mom must have detected my guilt those last two days. That explained why she had looked at me with so much disappointment and concern this morning. She knew if she didn't do something to help me release the guilt, she would have a hard time crossing over to the spirit world, or maybe she even thought I wouldn't be able to let her go. Regardless, my siblings reassured me, their little brother, that I had made the right decision.

This experience exposed me to an understanding about the negative impact of guilt. I realized that the conscience is the tool that tries to guide us to make good and valuable decisions. Guilt is nothing more than a method of control, a feeling that keeps us from moving forward. It keeps us paralyzed. What was there really to fear? Fear not.

I promised them and declared to myself that from that day forward I would never allow myself to operate from a position of guilt. I had gotten the message, and I would listen. Mom's message, and the feeling that she was literally within me, was such a clear vision I will never forget it. The guilt I had taken on had completely dissolved, and no matter what happened in my life, from that day forward it would never come back. I was certain that my full abilities would return by morning.

To my great relief I was gradually getting the feeling back in my body. I felt a tingling sensation creep slowly up my legs and arms and move down my torso. When the feeling met in the middle of my body, the paralysis that had kept me pinned disappeared. I shook my head and said out loud, "Mom, you weren't going to remove the paralysis until I told everyone, isn't that right?" I wasn't surprised that Mom was not going to free me until I freed myself from guilt. I still, to this day, thank her for her insistence and that awakening. While everyone was still in the room, I mentioned to them that I wanted to go back to Williston, North Dakota the next day to start making arrangements for Mom's funeral. A couple of my sisters decided to come along.

My brother had to gently support me on my way to the restroom—although I could walk, I was still weak—but thankfully he did not have to accompany me. I had gained a deeper understanding of how Mom was feeling now in her hospital bed because I had experienced the same thing, if only for a short time.

Mom had prepared her children during the past years by assuring us she was at peace with the inevitability of death. We had assured her of our own acceptance as well. When the end came, however, it was only her children who did not want to face the inevitable. What was it we feared?

I lay down again to regain my stamina. I drifted towards sleep with thoughts of how wonderful Mother was, how she had always been there to offer kind words of inspiration and encouragement. That she had been certain to take care of her kids up to the last minute, to offer guidance without interference, was a true gift for her children. She never liked to see anyone in pain, so thoughtful, so loving. I fell asleep knowing that in the morning I would say goodbye to Mom, and then I would leave for the ranch in North Dakota. Content with those plans, I actually got a few hours of really good sleep.

Chapter Eleven

Healing in Undreamed of Ways

Bright and early Tuesday morning, Mom's nurse came to administer a little morphine and soothe her with a sponge bath. The nurse asked my sister if the family members would like handprints and a lock of Mom's hair. Mom had made a comment just a week earlier that she wanted to get her hair cut, my sister remembered.

A little while later, Mom's oxygen level dropped from 80 to 50, and she began to break into a sweat. A few of my sisters were there with her when the nurse came back to administer a little more morphine to ease her discomfort.

Meanwhile, I woke that morning feeling a little weakened from the past five days. Still, the night's sleep had done me a world of good. I felt my energy returning. I wiped my eyes and saw my sister resting in the other bed and quietly informed her that I was going to take a shower. The water was warm and invigorating. I was excited to go over and see Mom.

She and I had a special bond now more than ever, and I wanted to see her one last time. I quickened the pace, jumped out and quickly dressed, and walked next door to grab a muffin and some milk for my sister and me.

Back in the room while sitting at the small table, I began to feel a bit odd, thinned and transparent. I got myself to the bed and lay down diagonally just to rest. Within seconds I had lost feeling again from the waist down. I said aloud, "Mom, I got the message last night. Why is this happening again?"

Char peeked her head around the corner from the bathroom to check on me. I told her I couldn't feel my legs again. She continued to get ready. I supposed maybe she thought I was just moving too fast after such a big day yesterday. She reappeared in the bedroom and told me to rest while she went about loading bags into the car.

Donna came in soon after. She panicked a bit and asked if I was okay. I was having a very hard time catching my breath. I told her I was feeling both light-headedness and a kind of heaviness. When she came closer to inspect, it was obvious that I was struggling to breathe.

"What do you want me to do, Tom? Should I call 911? Tom, what should I do? Please tell me!"

"Please just sit with me and hold my hand. This is something I have to go through. But promise me you won't leave."

She sat down and held my hand. I could see she was scared. I lay there incapacitated. My sister was crying and holding my hand. I didn't realize that my body looked to be in so much agony. My chest heaved up and down like something was trying to get out of it, while my upper torso looked as though it was levitating off the bed. Char had returned to find this scene and met her sister's gaze with an unquestionable shared fear.

I gasped as I told them I was having a hard time getting enough air. I began taking very short, pressed breaths. My voice became quite shallow, and all the while I was losing sensation in my legs again. My sisters began to massage them, trying to get the circulation back and hoping to keep me conscious. Another sister entered and took one look at the three of us. Sandi clearly had a difficult time putting the pieces together.

I felt a wave of heat start from my core, and I instinctively lifted my shirt and fanned myself. It felt like I was on fire. Sandi opened a window and got a wet washcloth to try to cool me down. I felt extreme pain in my abdomen and was barely able to speak due to the lack of oxygen, but I managed to ask them to call the hospital and see how Mom was doing. My sister dialed another sister at the Mayo Clinic across the street on her cell phone. She learned that Mom's oxygen had just dropped from 80 to 50.

I wasn't able to actually hold the phone at this point. My body was surrendering to another bout of paralysis. I continued trying to voice my concern for Mom, but to no avail. I no longer had control of my speech. I couldn't get another word out. I was less scared, though, than the day before, when I had been completely unsure of what was happening. I lay there on the bed, barely breathing but able to hear the panic and conversation between my sisters on the phone, one reporting blow-by-blow what was happening with Mom, the other relating what was happening with me.

It was obvious that we were linked together somehow, Mom and I. Everything was happening to both of us during the same time frame. Mom's oxygen had dropped about the same time my breathing became laborious. When I felt extreme heat and became sweaty, followed by a sense of numbed relief, Mom had just been administered another dose of morphine. Char commented to Donna that the only part of me that then actually looked afflicted in any way was my hand, which appeared crippled and withdrawn, as though I had suffered for years with severe arthritis. It looked like Mom's.

My niece had just arrived in the room from Mom's, my sister having asked her to go and see if she could help heal me. Everyone was concerned. My mother's body was shutting down, and mine seemed to be tagging along for the ride. Still, I felt in no mortal danger.

My niece's husband had suffered a bad accident some time ago, and she had studied some healing techniques to apply to him at home due to distance from a hospital and capping out on treatment possibilities. She began to run her hands up and down about six inches above my legs. I tried to tell her to be patient, that I was okay and not to worry. I felt fine—never mind that I couldn't speak or move my body.

I was feeling more relaxed, and I could hear them all taking account of it, probably the transference effects of the morphine. My eyes closed, I was lying there completely relaxed, not a care in the world. I could still hear everything going on around me. There were five of them now in the room with me. They mentioned that my eyes, still shut, were moving very rapidly from side to side and up and down as though I was seeing something.

It was true. The most remarkable thing was unfolding. I was in a state of complete relaxation, prevented from moving a muscle, both from the paralysis and apparently the effects of my mother's last dose of morphine. Then it came steadily closer—an extremely bright white light. I immediately tried to open my eyes and tell everyone in the room what I was seeing. It didn't click in. Regardless of how alert I felt to both the light and my family in the room with me, I was unable to open my eyes or speak.

However, I was not afraid, either of the light or of having no control over my body, until I tried to do things without response from my body. I began to get a little worried, and the light disappeared as though it was being pulled out of a funnel. My focus shifted from concern to intrigue. I lay there trying to figure out what I had just seen. I tried once again to open my eyes and speak. Still no success. I quickly took a physical inventory and decided that I was feeling okay; at least I was not in any pain.

Then it happened again. An intense illumination so intense came toward me, as though it had just emerged through the tiny end of a tear in the fabric of time and space. It came more intensely than the first time.

I lay there desperately trying to open my eyes, but I couldn't. I tried to speak, but still had no control. And then the light disappeared back to where it had come from. In amazement, I lay there trying to make sense of what I was experiencing. Clearly I was in a space and time between worlds. I had no ability to use my body or my conscious mind. If I had, it would have been all too obvious what was happening. The light was clear and intense; it was the light to eternal life.

I thought that it wouldn't happen again, and any minute I would be able to open my eyes and speak. But no sooner did I have the thought than the light came again for the third time. The intensity was beyond measure. But in my mind's eye, I found no discomfort in looking at it directly. It was in fact alluring and felt light. I took it in gratefully. And then again, it disappeared.

Karen came barging in with a delivery from Mom's room, and she handed a piece of paper to Donna. Donna examined the paper and held it to her chest for a few seconds, tears streaming from her face.

"Tom, this is Mom's handprint."

I was far from them at the time; only a trace of me remained in the room. I did not hear what she had said to me. The events that were unfolding were unexplainable.

Instinctively, Donna lifted my hand and laid it on Mom's handprint atop my chest. At the very contact with the paper, the light returned with such force that I could not deny what it was. It was indeed the light to eternal life, and it seemed to be looking for me. Its light held the keys to every beautiful word spoken on the earth. How entrancing and radiant it was. All thoughts of fear and uncertainty disappeared from my mind. I had never felt as connected to anything or anyone as I did to the light, completely safe and embraced in love. With my hand on my mom's handprint and my eyes still shut, my mother appeared right in front of me. We held hands and faced each other.

What I can only describe as a non-painless, electrical force of power shot up my left arm, across my chest and down my right arm. I could actually see the current leave my right hand and enter my mother's left hand, then shoot up her left arm, across her chest and down to her right hand. We were joined together, facing each other, linked as this source circled through our bodies three times.

My family watched in amazement as they laid my hand on the handprint and my body was immediately jolted, a sight to make one's hair stand on end. It looked as though I were being electrocuted. Regardless, a sense of peace was filling the room. It lasted about a minute, and then my body began to calm down.

The circling energy traveled through the two of us a fourth time before I let go of her right hand, still holding on to her left. She stood slightly behind me, and the light came again with such purpose that I knew exactly where we were going. There was no sense of time as we know it on this planet, only to say that the speed and smoothness with which we seemed to be traveling were a marvel. Before I knew it, my mom and I were both on the other side and were standing in what seemed a bright and vast room without walls.

My mom and I were still holding hands; we spoke not a word, our eyes wide with the wonder of what was before us. My father and my grandparents, my mother's parents, were standing to the right of me. I gasped at the sight of them, because it was real. I knew I wasn't dreaming. I knew where we were.

The place shone bright and emitted the most remarkable sense of love. We were welcomed through what felt, to me, like a vibration permeating through every cell of my being. In my forty years I had never experienced such a clear sense of peace and love. It was truly wondrous. Beyond the love that was present, I felt as though every answer to every question was at my grasp had I asked. Things I did not understand in my life became clear. It was as though my mind had expanded to comprehend millions of thoughts, ideas and paradigms simultaneously.

Where these thoughts came from, I cannot say. But I can say it was as easy as brushing teeth or driving a car after you've been doing it for ten years. It just happened—some form of telepathy. I found this fascinating, as I was clearly unable to manage this feat on earth. Of all the thoughts that were flying into my head, two subjects I found most interesting. There was the awareness of pure love, thoughts and prayers for all of us. There was not one who was left out, not one. If we only could feel a minute amount of the love that is felt for us, I am convinced we would not struggle as we do today. There was so much love.

I was astounded to see a staircase positioned between my dad and my grandparents. As I stood there in amazement, just taking it all in, it never occurred to me that I was dead. In fact, I was not dead. I had not passed. My body was back in the hotel room being tended to by my sisters. Somehow I understood that I had been granted this visit, the chance to escort my mom to heaven. There was a reason for me to be here.

The staircase brought with it clarity as to what we aspire to learn and gain while on earth. We are some of the bravest souls to go there, to forget all of this wonder, this space of love and acceptance. Still, I was here to see and experience heaven. There were obvious levels to this place, if it can even be called such, hence the stairway. The knowledge imparted to me was to encourage others to gain in understanding, to treat themselves, others and the earth with compassion and kindness.

I gently tugged on my mom's right hand and guided her in a sweeping motion toward my father and her parents. I watched her gracefully move toward them. She greeted them and proceeded to glide up the staircase. She arrived at the top and turned around to face us. She was a vision. She had the biggest smile on her face, and she was the woman in the photo at our farmhouse—no more than twenty-four years old, beautiful, young, full of life. There was always something different about that photo. I had searched for a meaning in that photo for decades. The original hangs in my home to this day.

As I looked up at my mother smiling down at me, standing at the top of the staircase, I knew at that point what I had to do. A message came directly into my soul that I needed to share this experience. The message for everyone is that we are all loved unconditionally, and it is important for people to have a better understanding about what happens to us after we leave the physical world. Passing really isn't a death, but a new beginning.

Back in the hospital, it was obvious to my sister that Mom and I were somehow connected. I was experiencing everything in the hotel across the street that my mother was experiencing in her room in the Mayo Clinic. "Tommy is going to bring you to the light so you can cross over. He can't go through forever with you. You have to let him come back."

It appeared the purpose was twofold: one, to show me truth and eliminate my pointless fear of death; and two, for me to tell my story, and bring peace and hope to others who have already lost someone. This place was beyond comprehension, even though when we arrive it all feels natural and we all feel a sense of belonging and of home like no other.

Only after I had returned from the light, conscious and aware, was I able to open my eyes and speak. When I did open my eyes after a bit, I was looking straight up to the heavens. I began speaking in a low, muffled tone. "I saw the light, I saw the light. It was so bright and beautiful. I saw the light."

They gasped at what they heard. "She's so beautiful, Mom, she's beautiful, she's smiling at me," I continued. For although I had returned, as I stared up I could see directly into the heavens. I could still see our mother looking down at us. Tears were running from the corners of my eyes and onto the bed.

"She's beautiful," I continued, "she's beautiful. She turned around and smiled at me with the biggest smile, she's twenty-four years old again, she's just beautiful." I explained to them that we had seen Dad and her parents when we crossed over to the other side. Mom had always talked about being young again and how she would give anything just to be forty again. She now had her wish, and with so much peace and comfort. After settling a bit more in my body, I started to describe the journey to my family.

You're home now, Mom.

Mom's soul or spirit had just crossed over, but we were all unsure if her body was still alive. Someone ran over to find out. Upon entering the room they asked Barb how Mom was holding up. She reported that Mom was resting very peacefully, the most peaceful she'd seen her in days.

Chapter Twelve

Choices and Decisions

Before everyone left the room, I made mention that I didn't need to go back over to the hospital to say goodbye to Mom like I had planned earlier. This idea felt foolish now, since I had been gifted with the privilege of escorting Mom to heaven myself. I told everyone I had just left her in the most incredible place, and I had no need to see her body shutting down. I had seen more than I had ever imagined I would. Mom had been with us right up to the end, making sure we all understood what was happening to us in the afterlife. I pondered how this knowledge could change life forever. My faith was renewed.

My brother and four sisters stayed with Mom for the next eighteen hours while her organs proceeded to shut down. The rest of us began the fourteen-hour drive back to the farm house. Knowing there were so many of my siblings still with Mom gave me a reassuring sense of peace. I knew in my heart that the body in that bed was only a shell of her, and it would be just a matter of time before it passed on. She was as comfortable as she could be. The morphine was keeping her pain free.

I kept thinking of the place I had left her. I sat for long quiet hours remembering the intensity of pure love I had felt in heaven, how happy she was now, how grateful I was and how much love I felt for her, and grateful for being able to see my family, my dad. I was becoming re-grounded in my own body from the journey, and what had occurred was really beginning to sink in.

Had Dad come that night all those years ago to tell me about this? That I would be okay? That occurrence had happened at a time when I was wondering if he would be proud of me, if I had made the right choices in my life. I thought he was coming to let me know that I had, but just maybe providing insight to that situation had also allowed him to prepare me somehow for this. I shook my head in utter amazement. For what is in the mind of God is but a mystery. It is just better to love and be at peace with others.

Shortly after we had left the hospital, Mom was moved to a different floor. They had more critical care patients being flown in and needed the room. Even this situation was a message that it was time to move on. The new floor, under partial construction, just didn't feel the same. The emphasis had shifted.

And yet, the concept of "under construction" fit well with what I had learned from heaven, for we are all under construction. The evidence is the feeling of discontent and separation from our Father that we have here. We live our lives in search of fulfillment, when we have it already. We are looking in the wrong places. It isn't that our pursuits are wrong; they are just experiences. But somehow, when we get to this place and time, we forget where we came from, who we truly are.

Why is that? I wondered. No matter for now. I had come back from heaven awake, gifted beyond comprehension and prepared to share with others who are struggling, as I had, with the idea of death.

Back at the hospital, Mom's body was lingering. All the while, my family never left her alone. A caring relative suggested they leave the room at one point, as she probably wouldn't take her last breath while they were there. They were advised to tell her they'd be back in an hour or so and leave the room.

We first drove to Char's home. It had been far too long and too much had occurred since she had spent time with her husband. We shared the details of our experience earlier that morning with her family. Her joy was returning in being with her family, but I could tell her thoughts were still with Mom. We stayed the night, although no one slept very well knowing that Mom was passing away.

It was 4:20 a.m. when the nurse at the hospital tapped my sister Marilyn on the shoulder to let her know that Mom had passed on. When the phone rang at Char's just minutes later, we all knew what it meant.

Chapter Thirteen

Keep Only the Lessons
and the Love

The trip to Williston was quiet, each of us perhaps a little numb from the past days' events. Knowing we were all coming together in Williston to bury our mother was difficult for everyone. The awareness that Mom had slipped away from us was beginning to set in. Although we were very grateful to learn where she had gone, the realization that we would not be able to hug our mother again felt too permanent.

We arrived at the farmhouse that our mother had lived in for the last forty years of her life. We arrived in the evening and the house felt cold and lonely, strangely empty without her. I entered the home that I had grown up in, in a state of disbelief that Mom was really gone. I walked around the house for hours, looking at everything that she had collected in her home.

My eyes were constantly drawn to all the spiritual items, the crosses, pictures of Jesus, statues of Mary…

it went on and on. Her faith had not only endured after my father's passing, it had strengthened. Mom had created a piece of heaven here at the farmhouse, and it gave me such a sense of peace that, despite her being alone for so many years, she had felt safe in that farmhouse. She clearly had God on her side. Everything was coming into focus as I walked around for nearly four hours, looking in each room and examining each item carefully. Each one had held meaning for Mom.

It was eleven that evening when I finally sat down and visited with the rest of my family. I remember we spoke of her faith. I understood that it was beyond question. I didn't realize that it was beyond measure until I had been in her home and seen for myself what she had brought close to her in her sacred space.

As a boy I had always felt spiritual, but I did not feel drawn to church. My belief in God or a higher power was absolute and without question. I knew this to be true on faith alone. Although I had questioned God after my father's death, my questions were completely resolved during my mother's passing.

I became aware of two distinct feelings. The separation from heaven had left me feeling alone, and also with a responsibility to share this experience. Fear was beginning to take hold in a different way. Now that I had made this commitment, I wasn't sure that anyone would understand, or worse—what if they didn't believe me?

Daily I thanked God for my mother and for allowing me to help her to the other side. Daily I still thank God for letting me feel the unconditional love, peace and joy that is waiting for all of us when we make our transition. As I thanked God for these gifts of experience, I continued hearing in the back of my mind that I needed to share our journey at her funeral.

Her reassuring voice echoed in my mind, encouraging me to be brave and to have faith. She knew within herself that if people heard of this journey, it might bring a quality and peace to their lives, and perhaps death would become a little easier to live with.

I tried to fight what I was hearing in my head. I had stuttered terribly as a child. What if under the pressure of speaking at the funeral, it came back to me in front of so many people —and in the Catholic church? What if I couldn't communicate clearly?

There were still many things to do before Mom's memorial service. We renamed the event "The Day We Celebrated Colette Lukenbill's Life." The day came when we had to meet with the funeral director. I had gone to high school with him. I asked him if we could have our niece, Jacinda, sing the song "Wind Beneath My Wings." The words in that song have such great meaning to me on how I felt about Mom. We were informed by the church that the song would be fine, but it had to be sung before she was taken down in front of the church because the song wasn't a traditional Catholic hymn.

The meeting was expectedly heavy, but as we concluded one of my sisters asked if we could have Mom's granddaughter, Karly, play her favorite song as they took her out of the church.

"I don't think that'll be a problem." The director was making notes on a piece of paper. "I just need the title of the song."

" 'Dance to the Polka,' " Char said. "That was her favorite song."

He looked away from his piece of paper—I'm sure trying not to laugh—and smiled. Our intention for this song was to try to uplift the congregation as they proceeded from the church service. We did not want people to leave with a heavy heart. He understood what we were trying to accomplish. He looked down at his notes and wrote as he said, "Polka out."

We all laughed. I knew at that moment our mother was so proud of us. She understood how we wanted to lift spirits as all exited the service and continued on with their lives.

It was time to pick out the casket. I'll be honest: even with all that I had been privileged to experience and see, this was very difficult for me. I wanted to get out of there as quickly as possible. After thirty minutes, we had picked out a beautiful soft pink casket lined with a fabric decorated with delicate pink roses. Mom had loved roses so.

The rest of that day was spent talking with the family. There were special things in the house that we had each bought Mom over the years. We knew with no one living at the farmhouse, we would need to take the time to locate any of these special treasures and take them back with us to our homes. Throughout the next few days I gathered up all of Mom's spiritual mementoes and distributed them with an instinctive message for the family members. It was the strangest thing for me to experience this, as I had never been able to do this in the past. I was only beginning to discover the changes in me as a result of my journey with Mom.

I would hand someone something and begin to talk to them like I was Mom. I found this most unusual, but somehow natural. It was such a moving and spiritual time for all of her children. I know everyone cherishes the items they received that day as selected especially for them and for Mom's own reasons. I have since been to each of their homes and noticed their gifts on display in some way.

Mom's wish had been to be laid to rest in her purple robe, which we all still felt a little funny about. We bought into the traditional custom to dress the deceased as if she were going to a very formal event. But many of my sisters had heard Mom say, "Why do I need to wear a dress? I'm just going to be sleeping anyway." In the end, we decided she was right. She was already where she needed to be, and that had nothing whatsoever to do with how she was dressed in a coffin. She wanted her purple robe, so the purple robe it was to be.

We began the task of cleaning out her closet. Right where the robe used to hang, there was a piece of masking tape lying on the ground. It read, To be buried with me in the casket. Mom had taken the robe with her to Minnesota. We all thought it was serendipitous that the piece of tape would have fallen off and landed on the ground where it did. There was no doubt that it was the right thing to put Mom in her purple housecoat. Of course, she'd need a purple nightgown to go under her robe. Barb and a few sisters went off to town to shop.

Chapter Fourteen

Lift Your Energy

It was the morning of the viewing. I didn't really want to go to the viewing, but I went with my brother to spend time with him. I had a hard time looking at Mom in the casket. The last time I had really seen her was on Tuesday morning when she and I had made the journey together to the other side. When she turned around and looked at me with that big smile, so vibrant and radiant, this corporeal body held no meaning to me other than a gift from God to experience the physical life. It is not who we really are.

That evening we held the Rosary as is customary in our faith. I wanted, once again, to be strong for my family. The funeral home began to fill with people. I was sitting in the front pew fifteen feet away from my mother's casket. At the Rosary it came to me how wonderful it was to be so close to her. The Rosary prayer takes about an hour and is conducted in a kneeling position. I was so busy with the event that I didn't think to sit in the second row, where there was a padded kneeling bench. Of course this came to mind as soon as I felt the cement floor, covered only with carpet, under my knees. I had to laugh to myself.

I honestly don't remember a lot of what the priest said. The pain in my knees was becoming unbearable. I began shifting my weight from side to side, trying to relieve the pain. I looked over at my sister for any suggestion she could silently offer. Here we were, trying to be so strong and bold, sitting in the front row, yet causing ourselves undue pain. I thought about how much pain Mom must have been in those last few years from her arthritis. She had tried to explain to us how the pain would become so intense that it would paralyze her. I could not comprehend this at the time, but I could certainly relate now.

I could tell my sister was feeling the same thing, because we were now breaking a sweat. I kept shifting my weight from side to side to find some relief. I could stand it no more and scooted my rear onto the pew just enough to relieve about half of the pain. My sister followed suit. The Rosary ended and the pain subsided as I sat back down on the pew.

It was the time for those who wanted to offer any words to come up to the front. A sister wanted to speak and motioned for me to go with her for moral support. When we stood at the front facing everyone,

I was happy to see that all of Mom's siblings were present. There were so many there to pay their respects. While standing with my sister, I once again could feel the worry in my heart about disclosing such an intimate experience to everyone at the service the next day. But I put this aside, reminding myself that everything is done for a reason.

The risk of exposing my beliefs to the potential judgment and criticism of others was necessary. Interestingly, if I had known how the day would unfold I would have looked forward to it. Instead, my own judgments about how people might react prevented me from being in the present moment. Honesty is the best medicine, my inner voice of reason said clearly. Earlier in my life, I had always tried to live by this credo. All I had to do was to be open and honest. It was not my responsibility to make them believe. God needed no defense; He simply is. With that clear, I knew I couldn't fail.

The morning progressed, and soon it was time to get ready and go to the final ceremony. We headed into town and gathered at the Catholic church. So many people showed up that it started to make me a little nervous again about speaking. I successfully calmed my nerves by visiting with many of the relatives I hadn't seen in years.

The church filled quickly. The children and grandchildren were advised to wait in the back of the church with Mom until everyone was seated and the priest said an opening prayer. Just before the casket was rolled to the front, the song "Wind Beneath My Wings" was heard.

Tears were in our eyes as we watched the funeral director close the coffin and lay a cloth gently over it. I struggled with the idea of not being able to hug my mom again, but I could hear what she would say: "You know where I am. You were shown the way. Be happy for me. I now have eternal life with peace and joy, and without pain."

I thanked her for the reminder and started praying for the strength to get through the eulogy without breaking down. We settled in our seats and began to listen to the service. The congregation sang beautiful hymns. My sister Karen had declared that whatever page the Bible fell open to, she would find the perfect verse there to share with Mom's friends and family, and that she would then vow to live her life by it. Proverbs 6:2, verse eight was read: Trust in God at all times, my people. Pour out your heart before Him: God is a refuge for us. It felt like a message for me to relax and have confidence in what I was about to share.

I watched my mother's friends as they received Communion, and something came over me. I knew my purpose today was to share with the older generations my journey with Mom. I hoped to reassure them that they had so much to look forward to when their time came.

After Communion ended, it was my turn. I took a deep breath and walked to the front of the church and up the stairs to the podium. I immediately told everyone that the reason I was not going to be looking into the crowd was because I had brought a picture of my mother and her handprint up front with me, and I found comfort in any part of her that remained with me. I shared with them that I needed to draw strength to get through this without breaking down.

There were a couple of times that I had to stop talking because an overwhelming feeling took hold of me. I quietly took a moment and prayed to God to recompose me as quickly as possible; it worked every time. As I spoke of the journey, I could feel the love in the room. The risk was worth it. With all the emotion and honesty that was pouring out of me, there was not a dry eye as they absorbed my experience. I could feel the fear melting away from me, and I believe from them also. The greatest delight and surprise was to see the priest with a look of astonishment and approval. I continued with my journey as if I was reliving every moment.

The service came to a close, and Grandma's favorite song began to play as the guests gathered their thoughts and left the service. We could see the lightness in everyone's step and the smiles on their faces as they left their pews to the sound of the polka. The family was the first out of the church with Mom, and we watched over her as her casket was loaded into the first car.

I was standing outside the front of the church, my back to the large brick wall for support, when the priest walked over to me and shook my hand. "You did an incredible job," he said.

I was instantly so relieved. One of my biggest fears about sharing my story was that it had to be done in the Catholic church. My mother had known Father for years. One of my uncles also came up to me and thanked me for sharing my story. "Father also gave me his blessing for what I had shared," I told him.

We loaded into the limos and proceeded slowly to the cemetery, where I laid a final rose on Mother's coffin. She was gone.

There was a nice luncheon held at the church after the funeral. There were so many people there I hadn't seen for years. They were so loving and caring, and I enjoyed hearing about what they had been up to over the years and receiving confirmation that what I had shared was valuable to them.

Chapter Fifteen

Visions and Energy

After our mom's funeral, many of Mom's brothers and sisters came out to the ranch. We all sat around and visited for hours. All of my mom's relatives are so kind and thoughtful. My mother was the oldest of fourteen children. All the siblings were very close.

My youngest sister and I were in my mother's bedroom visiting and digesting what had happened in the last couple of weeks. We were in there for quite a while when one of my mother's sisters came in and started talking with us. She told us stories about when they used to go out dancing, mentioning that our mother was such a good dancer. She would get on the dance floor and a lot of people would just stand around and watch. She shared a few other stories with us, and it was really nice to hear the stories on this day. The love that I felt in this family was incredible, and I still cherish it every day.

While the three of us were reminiscing, my energy was being drawn to the corner of the room. I tried not to take my focus off my aunt, who was telling another story at the time, but the pull that was happening to me was incredible. I did everything in my power not to look to the left, but for one quick moment I just turned my head to see that there was a beautiful bouquet of red roses on the small table in the corner of the room. I quickly turned my focus back to my aunt and enjoyed the story that she was telling. All the while, I was being constantly pulled in the direction of the bouquet. I didn't understand what was coming from the corner of the room, yet I felt at that moment that I really didn't need to understand anything. I just let what was happening happen.

When my aunt had finished her story, the three of us just sat there for a moment. All of a sudden my aunt very slowly turned her attention to the bouquet of flowers and commented on how beautiful they were. They looked so real, but they were made out of silk. She was mesmerized by their beauty, and she slowly reached out her hand to touch a petal on one of the roses. As she slowly brought her hand closer to the petal, I saw my mother's hand come out of the bouquet and touch my aunt's ever so gently. I couldn't speak.

I knew at that moment I needed to give that bouquet of roses to my aunt. When I told her that I would like her to have the bouquet, I saw tears in her eyes.

I knew at that moment that she might have felt that touch from my mother. She was so grateful for such a small token. I was thrilled.

About six months later, I saw my aunt again on a trip back to the Midwest, and she mentioned how she had placed the bouquet of roses in her bedroom so it was the first thing she saw every morning when she woke up. I know at some level she feels my mother's energy with those flowers, and it helps her to get through her day.

During the first year following my mother's passing, the aunt with the roses sent me a few ads from magazines interested in publishing stories about abnormal experiences. Many times I pondered sending them a brief outline of my story, but I knew that I was going to put it in a book form someday instead. I still have those small magazine ads. Even my aunt must have thought that my story that I had shared at the funeral was substantial enough to have it published.

The next year of my life was not only very difficult in many ways, but also very rewarding. I was not only grieving the loss of my mother, but I was also grieving that I could not stay on the other side with my parents. That may sound odd to many, but to me it made total sense. What I had felt and witnessed that day back in March of 2004 was something that will stay with me forever.

I moved in and out of depression for about a year. A couple of things were very heavy on my mind. I was feeling very alone because of the journey I had experienced with my mother, and I was feeling very obligated to share my story. I felt I had been given a gift, and it would be selfish of me to keep it to myself. How was I going to explain something so extraordinary and have it make sense to the general population?

I struggled with the thought of writing a book and sharing something as personal as my mother's death while potentially reaping a financial reward from publishing the book. My ego completely got in the way and tried to make me feel guilty about sharing something so wonderful. I struggled with this for about a year before finally coming to the conclusion that it was okay to share the experience, as it would assist those who had questions about death and possibly make them feel at peace. I was now committed in my mind that a book was going to happen.

During the next year, many things happened that were blessings. The forty-minute drive back and forth to work gave me much time to reflect on my life. I was driving one day with a friend when something interesting happened. We didn't have the radio on that day for some reason. Abruptly I asked him if he had heard a sound. He responded, "No, I haven't heard anything." I very clearly was hearing voices once again in my truck. It sounded like four or five people having a very important conversation. My friend hadn't heard a thing, but to me it was very clear that people—angels, perhaps—were having a conversation.

I sat there in amazement for a long time and was mesmerized by the clarity of their voices. It had been years since I had heard such a clear conversation. Were there many other times in my life it had happened and I just wasn't paying attention, or was there something happening or coming up in my life that was so important that an army of angels were surrounding me for my protection?

Whatever the situation was, it comforted me knowing that there was a presence supporting what I was trying to do at this point in my life. I have never been ashamed of what goes on in my life or of sharing with someone that I hear conversations of other people in my head. These things have never bothered me. I've always felt it was normal.

There was one particular morning when I was in deep thought about my life and my family. The thoughts of my mother were so intense that I could feel her coming around. When a loved one's energy is close by, the feeling is undeniable. The drive was filled with thoughts of how I was going to share in a book the experience of crossing over that March day of 2004 in Rochester. I was questioning my ability and really was struggling with it. I began to pray about it and continued on my drive.

I was deep in prayer when I came around a corner and drove to the top of a long hill. In a mountainside in the far distance, my mother's face was looking at me. It startled me so much that I had to pull over to the side of the road. I kept looking straight ahead and seeing my mother's face smiling at me.

The experience completely overwhelmed me and gave me a sense of peace that I had the strength and endurance to put the book together. I called a couple of my sisters and told them what had just happened. They were all mesmerized by how things were continuing to happen around me. After a few minutes of meditation, I knew that I did have the strength to proceed on with this book as the vision of my mother slowly disappeared into the mountainside. I started driving once again in complete awe of why these visions were constantly given to me. I felt grateful for them, as the visions helped so much to get through the day.

It was time to go back home to North Dakota to start making plans for the ranch. After all eight kids arrived at the ranch, we congregated outside to discuss its future. Among eight siblings there are always eight different opinions, and sometimes it is difficult for us to come to an agreement. For me, all that was important was that we do the right thing for our family and to abide by my parents' wishes.

Our parents had clearly expressed their wish that the farm stay in the family. As a group, we discussed a price for the farmhouse so my brother could afford to buy it. Family discussions would always get a bit heated when money was the topic. However, I wanted all of us to get along and make this transition as smoothly as possible. I didn't want the fighting or bickering to continue between us.

I was feeling a little frustrated with the whole ordeal and decided to take a walk out in the pasture next to the house. It was my playground as a child. I would wander those hills for hours. At the top of one of the hills there were eight very large posts that were put in the ground years ago by my father. These posts were going to be used as a windbreak for our cattle from the cold snowy winds. We never had the money to complete the windbreak, so only the posts were there. I found myself weaving in and out of those eight posts. I felt as if those posts represented the eight children in our family.

On the top of one of the hills there were three large circles made out of rocks that resembled tepee rings. As a child, my sister and I used to play in these rings for hours. We never disturbed the rocks because we felt they had some sort of meaning. This day, I found myself looking at those tepee rings and praying for some guidance. Before I knew it, I wanted to build something very meaningful for the family and for my parents up on that hill.

The first thing that crossed my mind was that I wanted to build three crosses and put them in the middle of this large pile of rocks. Surveying the area, my eyes located a couple of scraps of wood, and I wandered over to them. There was some old rusty barbed wire in the same area. I assembled these two pieces of wood and proceeded to wrap the wire around them to make a cross. I walked over to the rock pile and lifted a rock. There was hole about a foot deep already there, so I placed the cross in that hole and propped a rock against it. I thought it was ironic that I didn't even need to dig a hole to set up this cross.

Wanting to build two more crosses, I looked around again and spotted some additional barbed wire and some lumber from old fence posts. With this material, I was able to assemble two more crosses. As I lifted another rock, there was once again a foot-deep hole to place the second cross in. I chuckled to myself and put a rock against the cross, and the cross stood firm and did not fall over. Assessing where I would like the third cross, I lifted another rock and to my surprise there was another foot-deep hole. I gently placed the end of the cross into the ground and propped the rock against it, and the third cross stood firm and did not tip over.

After the three crosses were completed, I looked at them and felt such powerful energy coming from what I had built. There was a cross for my father and one for my mother, and the third cross standing was for my siblings and me. The three crosses signified how strong our family was.

The next thing I was driven to do was to find three huge flat rocks, one to be used as a seat and the other two to place in front of it to signify an altar. I wanted to make a place that people could come and sit or kneel and pray if they chose to. I don't believe anything is a coincidence. I was able to find two perfectly flat rocks and assembled them accordingly. After making the altar, I took it upon myself to kneel and say a prayer for my family to provide us guidance during this time to perform the wishes of our parents. During my prayer, I thanked my parents for getting all of us to this phase of our lives. I also requested that they direct us in a way that they believed was best for us.

I knew I wasn't finished building what I want to call my "spiritual place," so I looked around and found an abundance of very small rocks. I decided to make two faces out of these rocks to resemble our parents. These faces were placed on the inside of the large circle around the outside edge. I continued to make what looked like arrowheads or birds flying, and I assembled the rocks accordingly to make eight figures.

After assembling the spiritual place, I sat there for what must have been an hour or so and then wandered back to the house. Everyone had known while I was gone to not bother me because they saw me working so diligently on the hill. When I got back to the house, I asked each person to come up individually after I returned to the top of the hill. I wanted them to share with me what they saw when they arrived.

I wandered back up to the top of the hill with a pen and pad in hand. I wanted to take notes and document each one of my sibling's feelings once they were able to view the spiritual place. Each arrived wondering what he or she was going see on top of the hill. There were many different reactions and feelings, which I think is a prime example of how everyone sees things differently and how we all have different opinions. No one is right or wrong, but it's how each of us interprets and views things.

It was a very special time for the family. After everyone had come up individually, I asked them all to approach as a group, and we shared what each had experienced from the spiritual place. I wanted everyone to hear the interpretations of others so that maybe all would realize that none of us are right or wrong, but are all entitled to our own opinions.

It was interesting to watch everyone's expressions when someone else was sharing his or her thoughts. It looked as if people were really trying to understand the other person's viewpoint. It was a nice way of assembling the family together. I asked everyone if they were open to a little exercise, and they all were. I had them walk down a pretty steep hill approximately 200 feet away. When we got to the bottom of the hill, I had everyone pick up a large rock, and I asked them to carry the rocks to the top of the hill and place them in the spiritual place wherever they chose. Everyone picked up a very large rock and proceeded one by one up the hill.

At the top of the hill, each person placed his or her rock on the mound around the crosses. I asked each one if he or she was interested in doing it one more time. They all agreed, and we walked back down the hill to get another rock for a second trip. During this trip, I could tell that people were getting a little tired and their energy level was falling. We got to the top of the hill once again and placed the rocks within the spiritual place accordingly. I looked around and said that a third time would be a charm.

Gradually everyone made it to the bottom of the hill for a third time and picked up a rock, and with some effort we all made it to the top once again and placed the rocks within the spiritual place. I wanted three trips to signify not only the individuals themselves, but also one rock for Mom, one for Dad and one for God. I believe these three had a very strong influence, and we needed to show them our appreciation and gratitude.

I feel that day was something special for everyone. I speak only for myself, but I felt a very strong energy that day on the hill. Everyone was so moved by the experience that we all wanted to take pictures individually of ourselves by the spiritual place. When the pictures were developed, we all had the surprise of our lives. Within a couple of the pictures, off to the right side of the three crosses was an image of a face. The closer we looked at the photo, the more all of us agreed that it was the face of a man.

The photo was so incredible that we e-mailed it around to the rest of the family, and everyone saw the image. I showed it to friends, and they were all amazed at what was on that photo. I love the fact that something occurred on that day that was so powerful that it tried to come through in a photo. People can make their own assessments of what they think the image is, but when you look closer at the photograph, to me there is no question. It is further validation of what has occurred frequently in my life.

I couldn't have been happier taking three hours to assemble the spiritual place, because in the hours following with my family, I believe it gave everyone a sense of peace. To this day when people go back to the ranch, we visit the spiritual place at the top of the hill, and it provides such comfort to all of us.

After a week at the ranch, we all headed back to our homes in different states. Everything was not resolved, but I felt we had accomplished enough that everyone was at ease. At home in California, I once again settled in to my routine, and like always was struggling with the idea of training horses for the rest of my life. I knew the book was something that I had to do, and it was always at the forefront of my thoughts. There was so much going on in my life that I had a huge challenge balancing it all. The old saying is that life must go on, and it does.

In September 2004, I decided to take a trip back to Rochester and the Mayo Clinic. I wanted to go back to talk to the doctors, nurses and anyone who was around me during my stay at the hospital. The night before the flight, I was very nervous about the trip and decided to give my sister Char a call. I called her three times with no answer. I went to bed that evening feeling very uneasy about the upcoming trip.

The next morning, Char returned my call. She informed me that after awakening she clearly remembered a dream she had had that night. She had dreamt that she had entered a room and saw our mother embracing me. Char recalled a very bright golden light in the background. Char also mentioned to Mom that I was really struggling and was going to need all the help and strength she could give me to have a very successful trip back to Rochester.

The morning of the flight was not only very exciting, but also a little nerve-wracking. Halfway through the flight to Minneapolis, I was listening to music on my headset and staring at the seat in front of me, when suddenly what I can only describe as a movie screen came in front of my face. Inside this screen, I witnessed children running through what seemed the most incredibly lush and vibrant green meadow that I had ever seen. I looked in amazement at the depth of color of every tree, shrub and flower that was shown to me.

After what seemed to be an eternity, but I am sure was only a few seconds, I focused once again on the two children, wanting to know who they were. In my mind, I kept calling out for them to get their attention. In an instant, I recognized the nine-year-old boy to be my cousin Kelly, who had drowned. I called out his name, and he turned around and smiled at me. I knew at that moment that for some reason I had crossed over again, and I tried to figure out why.

I asked Kelly who the little girl was that was with him, and he just smiled. My interest was piqued, and I kept asking him over and over again. At that moment, my mother showed up in the left side of the "movie screen." I was not surprised to see her and that she was very happy. I asked her who the little girl was, and I heard her say to me without opening her mouth that I knew who it was and that I just needed to look closer and focus. I chuckled and remarked that it would be easier if she would just tell me. She smiled back at me and insisted that I focus and think harder.

At that moment, I gasped and realized that the little girl was Megan, Kelly's niece, who had died at age eight of cancer. She was there with her uncle, playing in a meadow on the "other side." I began to gently cry, and I am sure that people sitting on either side of me in the plane thought I was a little crazy. I did not care what they thought, and I cherished that moment on the plane with my loved ones who had crossed over. Slowly the movie screen disappeared, and within an hour I had landed at my destination.

My sister Donna met me at the airport, and we had a two-hour drive to Rochester. I shared with her what had happened on the plane ride. We drove with feelings of excitement but also feelings of sadness. We were stirring up a lot of memories that were still very raw in both of us.

We arrived at the hotel where we had stayed during our mother's stay in the hospital. We quickly made our way to the front desk and asked if there were any rooms available. Luckily for us, there were, and we asked to stay in room 135. This was the room that we had occupied during our mother's stay at the hospital and the room in which I had had the profound journey with my mother.

Once in room 135, however, Donna and I looked at each other and knew that it was the room next door that we wanted and not the one we had requested. We made our way back downstairs and up to the front desk. We approached the hotel clerk and said that we were mistaken in the room that we had originally requested and that we would like the room next door. I asked if it was available. Fortunately it was, and we gladly swapped keys with Bob, the hotel clerk.

After he handed us the keys, I explained to Bob that we wanted this particular room because we had previously stayed in it six months ago. Bob said that he remembered us and he was surprised to see me walk into his hotel that evening. He then shared with me that he was the one who had called 911 and thought that I had possibly died of a heart attack later that evening because he never saw me again after I was rushed to the hospital. I thanked him for the room, and we made our way to it.

After a few minutes of relaxation, we decided to go down to the hotel restaurant to have a little bite to eat. We finished a light dinner and wandered back to the front desk. I asked Bob if he wouldn't mind jotting down on a piece of paper the memories he had of that evening six months ago. He looked at me and asked if I had crossed over with my mother.

My sister grabbed for the counter, because she'd become weak in the knees from what she had just heard. I also caught myself holding on to the counter for a little extra support. My sister and I looked at each other, and then I turned and looked at Bob and said to him, "Yes, Bob, I did. But how do you know that? You don't even know me."

"Oh no, son," he replied. "I have known you for a long, long time."

I couldn't speak, and I wasn't going to question what I had just heard. Then Bob said he would be more than happy to write down everything he remembered, but he had a huge favor to ask of me. He told me that his wife was very ill and that her days were numbered. She was at peace with dying, but only talked about what it was going to be like on the "other side." He wanted me to share my story with her at brunch the next morning. I was bewildered at what I had just heard and agreed to talk with him and his wife the next morning.

The next morning the four of us met in the hotel restaurant for coffee. Bob's wife was a very sweet woman, and I couldn't wait to tell her my story. Now I understood why the day before on the plane to Rochester I had been shown the scenery for the first time since crossing over with my mother. During the initial trip to the other side, all I had seen was gray and white, a staircase, my father and my mother's parents. There were no trees or landscaping during the crossing over with my mother, although today I can honestly articulate what you can expect to see when you cross over.

I shared with them the "movie screen" that had appeared to me and the experience that had occurred on the plane the day before. The validation that I needed was given to me in the form of seeing my cousin and his niece playing. I now understood what I was seeing again and was able to communicate it to others. I will never forget the look in their eyes as I shared my experiences with them.

At the conclusion of my story we all got up from the table, and I got the biggest hug from Bob's wife. She thanked me over and over for sharing the experience with her, because she wasn't afraid of dying but really wanted to know what it felt like and what it was going to look like when she crossed over. Their home, I was told, had a backyard that was incredible. It was their tropical paradise in the Midwest. She loved her backyard and was just hoping and praying that the other side had the look and feel of their tropical paradise and more. I explained to her in great depth and compassion that it has all of it times one million.

That meeting left me on cloud nine. The gift that I had received, not only in March, but also the day before on the plane ride, I had now shared with complete strangers and had touched them deeply. The rest of our trip went very well, and we found doctors, nurses, ambulance drivers and hotel staff to be very helpful, kind and informative. We left that trip feeling very hopeful and excited to return home. With written statements from those that were there with me six months ago in hand, I began my journey back home.

Christmas is a time for families to gather, and we had done so on several occasions. This year the holidays would be different because we were all going to gather for the first time without our mother present. All eight children had agreed to assemble at the ranch. One by one each of the eight families began to show up. The weather was normal for the Midwest that time of the year. The cold air reminded me of my youth when all of my older siblings would make the journey home for the holidays.

We all settled in at the farm and enjoyed each other's company. The Christmas dinner was cooking, and the pleasant heat from the woodburning stove was keeping the house very toasty. We all gathered around the kitchen table and enjoyed dinner. We laughed and told stories from our childhood and reminisced about our lives. It seemed a little strange that we were all there without the matriarch of the family. Life had changed, and the dynamics of the family were now shifting.

No one was in a big hurry to finish dinner, so we found ourselves eating very slowly. It was like life was in slow motion, and we were all hoping that this was just a dream. Dinner concluded, and one by one family members settled in to other rooms of the home. Instead of the normal gift exchange, we decided to just play a few games and the winners could choose a small gift. It was fun for everyone, and we found ourselves laughing for hours.

On this trip home, I had asked everyone to bring their stories with them that they had written about the time we had spent in the hospital in Rochester. I wanted everyone to share their stories with the rest of the family that Christmas. I thought it would be nice for the family to hear one another's feelings about where they were in their lives.

We all assembled in the living room, and one by one stories were read in no particular order. It was a very emotional experience to hear everyone's story. The energy and the peace in that room that evening were unbelievable.

I was sitting in the living room facing the wall where there were many pictures of our family. One of my nephews, Derek, was sitting beside me. As the stories were being read, I could sense that there was something going on with him. Throughout the evening, I would look over at Derek to ensure that he was doing okay. I could just sense from the energy that was coming from him that something profound was happening to him.

One of my sisters was reading a very touching story when something miraculous happened to my nephew. When we finished that evening, he asked me if I could come with him for a second, and I followed him into what used to be Mom's bedroom. We sat on the bed for a moment, and I asked him if he was okay. He looked at me in such a way that I knew he wanted to share something. I reassured him that everything was okay and that I would not judge him.

He began to open up and tell me what had happened in the living room. During the last story that was being read, something began to pull his attention to the large photograph of Grandma on the wall. During one part of the story he looked up at the photo, and he saw very clearly that Grandma was crying. He said he tried to shake it off as nothing and looked down for a moment. Clearing his mind, he looked up one more time and saw the exact same thing. The photograph of Grandma's smiling face was now a photo of her crying, not from sadness but from happiness. Seeing her family gathered together and sharing their stories had warmed her heart. He said that it stayed that way until the story had finished.

I told him that what he had just witnessed had actually happened and to never question it. Many people will probably tell him that this experience never occurred, that it was a figment of his imagination, but I know differently. I told him to embrace the moment and to never be afraid of something that seemed out of the ordinary. I feel he understood what I was saying, and to this day he is a very focused and determined young man.

I wish at his age I would have had the guts to talk to someone about what was happening to me in my life. Yet I feel I wasn't supposed to, because it was all a part of my learning process. I will never forget that Christmas for many reasons. The days flew by, and before we knew it we were all saying goodbye and heading back to our respective homes. It was very hard to leave knowing that I would probably not be visiting as often in the future.

We all want to believe that not only our pets, but all living creatures make it to the other side. I had always believed in my heart that this was true, and on one particular evening this belief was cemented in me for life. I had a cat that was very old and had to be put down. I made an appointment with a good friend who was a veterinarian to come to my home the next day and put my cat to sleep. I went to bed that evening very sad about losing the companionship of that wonderful cat. Yet I now fully understand dreams and what they mean.

That evening I had a dream. I was on a hilltop looking down on a group of about fifty children. Forty-nine of the children had pets in their laps, all except one little girl. My eyes were making their way around the fifty children when I spotted a couple of Rottweiler puppies. I looked very closely and called out their names. Lexus and Marcus, the Rottweiler puppies, turned and acknowledged me, and at that moment I knew once again where I had traveled while sleeping. Lexus and Marcus were two puppies that did not make it after birth. My spirit body had left my physical body and traveled to the other side to see that all pets cross over. I knew then that the little girl without the pet was the one waiting for my cat to arrive.

This was the first time that I had actually witnessed the other side while in a dream state. All the other times were in the middle of my day, while I was completely awake and functional. I awoke that morning feeling okay about letting my cat go. Knowing there was a little girl waiting anxiously for her, I said a prayer for my cat and allowed her to leave her very weak physical body and return as a very healthy animal on the other side. It is comforting to me and many others to know the final destination of our pets when they pass on.

On one occasion, I was traveling home from a horse show and was in deep thought about my mother. I missed her physical body not being on earth, but was grateful that her spirit body was around constantly. Driving down the freeway with my thoughts on Mother, I suddenly had a vision of her sitting in a rocking chair on a deck at my sister's house in Minnesota. She was watching Char plant flowers in a flower bed by the deck. I kept seeing this image of Mom rocking in the chair and enjoying the beautiful spring air and flowers that were around her that day. I drove in amazement of what I was seeing and couldn't figure out why this was happening.

A few minutes later, I decided to give my sister a call and ask her what she was up to. She told me that she was planting flowers in a new bed that she had built by the deck next to the guest house. Char also mentioned to me that she had dedicated this new flower bed to Mom. She explained how she had been talking to Mom while planting the flowers in the bed. She had a strong feeling that Mom's spirit was around that day and had the urge to keep chatting with her. I got emotional hearing her story, and when she finished I began to tell her about my experience of that day.

The amazing thing to both of us was the similarities in what was happening to us miles apart. When she heard the part about Mom being in the rocking chair on the deck, she was amazed. She shared how she had just moved the rocking chair from the garage to the guest house that morning. We were both so grateful for what had just happened that we felt Mom's spirit even stronger.

How do you explain these wonderful coincidences? Or are they not coincidences, just normal things that happen to everyone, although many don't pay attention? All I know is, for us it was what we needed at that point in our lives. We talked often about how much we loved our parents and how grateful we were to have them in our lives.

I continued through life training horses and trying to balance out my new profound experience. I have never closed myself off to things that may seem out of the ordinary.

My travels as part of horse training have brought me to many places. On one particular trip, I had a profound experience outside of my own family. A friend had just lost both parents a couple of months apart and was still grieving. I was minding my own business when something drew me up to the vendors at the horse show. I was walking slowly along the booths, when all of a sudden at this one particular booth I hit a very cold spot. I thought it was a little odd, but continued walking.

After walking about fifty feet, I sensed something telling me to turn around, and so I did. I continued walking back, and when I hit the same area again the cold spot was still present. I chalked it up to just the temperature in a building being different. I walked away, and once again a voice told me to turn around and come back. I try not to disappoint anyone, so I obliged and turned around.

When I hit that cold spot again, I was standing in front of a vendor who was selling many little stick pins. I looked down and fixed a stare on one tiny pin out of thousands. I lowered my head and looked more closely at the beautiful pin. It had a little figure of an angel on it. What or who was drawing me back to that pin? I knew then that something or someone was trying to get my attention. I walked away with a smile on my face, embracing what had just happened. Then I looked up into the vending area, and there were my friend's parents to the left of the vendors. My eyes welled up with tears, and I knew I had to say something to my friend about this experience.

I looked around and soon spotted my friend. As I approached her, she knew that I had something to share with her. My glassy eyes were all she needed to see to know something was up. I shared with her the experience of walking by the vendors and feeling the cold spot, not once or twice, but three times, and then being pulled to focus on one pin out of thousands, the pin of an angel. I then shared with her with no hesitation that her parents were here in spirit, watching her at the show.

She asked if they were still here, and I replied with a resounding "yes." I pointed to where her mother was sitting, her father standing behind her with his hands on her shoulders. She walked over to the area where I had directed her, pulled up a chair and sat next to her mother. To many it may have looked a little odd that she was talking to a chair, but to me it was very normal. I could tell she was very excited, yet emotional about what was happening. It was something that I had felt obligated to share.

A couple of months later at our world championships, my friend shared with me that she felt her mother's presence during one of her favorite events. I smiled back at her and acknowledged that she was absolutely right. I too felt her presence and was very happy that she knew her mother was still there in spirit.

I felt that my life at this point had made a turn and that it was going to be quite the journey. Needing a small vacation before the next big show, I traveled to the Midwest to spend a week with family on the lake. It had been a little over a year since our mother's passing, and time was definitely healing our pain from the loss. I arrived at the lake ready to relax.

Our days were filled with boating, fishing and swimming. I normally started my days with coffee and then a nice eye-opening shower. One particular morning, I was down for my morning shower and a feeling came over me. I couldn't explain exactly what the feeling was, but something was going on. There is something about water that really creates good energy around me. As I washed my hair, I suddenly had a vision of our mother sitting in a white plastic chair while my sister washed Mom's hair. I heard my mother express her gratitude for the kindness that she was feeling from her daughter.

As with my previous visions, I felt a little emotional and tried to analyze what I had just seen. I continued with my shower and then made my way upstairs. My family was sitting around having breakfast and drinking coffee. I was a little on the quiet side when I entered the room. After about ten minutes of my not speaking, my sister asked me what was wrong. I responded by saying "nothing" and that I was fine. After another ten minutes my sister commented, "I know you too well, and something is on your mind." She insisted that I open up.

After sitting at the table for a while, I decided to go ahead and tell her about the vision that had occurred in the shower. I explained to her about seeing my sister wash Mom's hair while Mom was sitting in a plastic chair. She looked at me a little funny and said, "Really?" She explained that the white plastic chair by the back door was the same one that would be brought into the shower to wash Mom's hair. She and Mom would have conversations about life, and Mom was always so grateful that she was being pampered by my sister. We were both amazed that things like this kept happening to me. I didn't want the visions to stop, but sometimes they were just a little overwhelming. They always stirred up a lot of memories and emotions.

The week went by very quickly, and before I knew it I was back home and off to the next horse show. It was really difficult for me to continue showing horses when I knew that deep down in my heart I was being drawn to write the book. It was very hard for me to balance work, writing and my personal life. Something always seemed like it was getting left behind.

Nonetheless, I was off once again to another location with customers and their horses. Packing up and driving to the next location seemed like such a waste of time at this point. Flying in and out and having someone else transport the horse seemed like a much better idea. But with no such luck, I was once again driving down the road to my next destination. The trip wasn't going to be that long. I was traveling to Las Vegas for yet another show.

I found myself doing a lot of meditation and praying along the way. I was trying to find the strength to start the process once again of writing this book. At this point in my life, I had started and then shredded the manuscript a couple of times. I knew in my heart it was what I was supposed to do, but my darn ego constantly got in the way.

This trip in particular was one that I will never forget. I was driving alone, and about halfway through the drive, I suddenly felt a presence in the passenger side of my vehicle. Out of the corner of my eye, I caught a glimpse of someone. My body stilled. I was trying not to look to my right. I stayed focused straight ahead on the road for another couple of miles. The individual that was sitting in my passenger seat was still there. I turned my head just enough to get a full view of the seat. My mother was in the truck with me. She was looking straight ahead, focusing on the road for me. At that point, I felt I could let go of the wheel and I would have gotten to my destination safely. But of course I didn't and proceeded down the road. I got a little shaken up from having her within three feet of me. I felt I needed to talk to a friend to tell her what was happening.

On the phone, before I could tell my friend what was happening, she knew something profound was going on just by the tone of my voice. I shared with her that my mother was sitting right there in the truck with me and I didn't know what to do. She laughed for a second and suggested that I should have a conversation with her. I don't know why I had become so nervous when I saw my mother. I felt that maybe it was just feelings of excitement. I knew her physical body had not been with us for over a year and a half, but her spirit body had always been around with a very strong presence.

My friend and I chatted for a few more minutes, and after she got me settled down, we hung up. I then had a conversation with my mom. It was a very exciting time, and yet a very emotional time. Of course, our conversation consisted of communication that was through vibration and energy, not words. As I have come to discover, all spirit bodies use energy to communicate, and if we pay attention we can very easily pick up what they are saying.

The longer my mother's presence stayed with me, the more relaxed I became. It was such an incredible feeling to have her with me for so long. After miles of driving, I got another shock. Not only was my mother present, but now my father had shown up as well. I had not seen him or heard from him in fourteen years. It was the first time that both of my parents had appeared. There was a very powerful message that my father wanted to share with me. He had messages for three of my siblings, and he knew I would pass the messages on. My trip to Las Vegas had become something out of this world. It was a very taxing show, to say the least, but I survived, and we all did well at the competition.

Back in California, my life continued on as normal. I got a phone call one day from a sister, and she had concerns for a gentleman who was in a coma and was holding on desperately. She asked if I thought it would be okay if she played my CD that I had produced earlier of the story of my experience in Rochester back in 2004. I advised that she contact the wife of the gentleman in the coma, and she did. The wife listened to it first and decided it would be very nice if they played it for him. The man was in hospice care, so knowing that he was at home was very comforting not only to him but to all involved.

My sister went to the home and quietly placed a CD player next to the man's bed. She turned on the CD and turned the volume just loud enough that she felt he would be able to hear it. The CD is 70 minutes long, and she said that there was a sense of peace that came over the room while it was playing. The CD finished, and my sister retrieved it and went back to her home. Less than twenty-four hours later, I was informed that the gentleman had let go and passed on.

Is it a coincidence or not? During the 24-hour period from when she told me she was going to play the CD for him and when he actually passed, I started getting a mysterious feeling in my home in California. Not thinking anything of it, I called a friend. She is what I want to call a spiritual life coach and has helped me in many ways these last five years. Before I could explain to her what my sister had done, she asked over the phone who the gentleman was who was standing behind my couch.

I jumped a little inside and said, "What?" She said that there was an unknown man who had shown up in my house and was lingering there. I mentioned what my sister had done the other day with the gentleman in the coma, and to my surprise my friend mentioned that his spirit body was lingering around me because of the CD and the information contained on it. She said it was a very easy fix and all we had to do was to explain to him that he had passed on and he needed to go to the light. I gently explained to the gentlemen that he had passed on and he was not to be afraid, and to just trust and pass into the light. He understood, and as fast as the feeling had arisen that he was in my home, he was gone.

It was years after my mother's passing that the most incredible experience happened. I was at work one day training horses, and something reminded me that I was to be getting a phone call at 11 a.m. I never ride with my phone on me because I have dropped it many times and stepped on it by accident. I have always had a very good sense of time, and that day was no exception. Promptly at 11 a.m I got in my car to check to see if anyone had called. There was no phone call yet, so I placed the phone back on the passenger seat.

Upon entering the car, I had one leg still out on the ground while the other was propped on the driver's side floorboard. After laying the phone down on the passenger seat, I slowly lifted my head and looked through the windshield. The parking lot faces my riding arena, and what I saw astonished me. Not more than thirty feet ahead of my car was a vision of my aunt, my mother's sister, who had been fighting cancer for years.

What was I seeing? My eyes were fixed on the vision of my aunt at that moment. She insisted that I focus on her bent knee. After I acknowledged her, she knelt to the ground, her arms outstretched. Two young children ran up to her: her son who had drowned at nine, and her granddaughter who had passed away from cancer at eight. I knew at that moment that my aunt had passed away, and I was once again witnessing what happens when we pass on. I couldn't take my eyes off the scene. After embracing the children, she stood up and the three of them walked hand-in-hand through my arena until they vanished at the far end.

I sat there in my car for a few moments, then got out slowly and made my way back to the barn. I continued working that day knowing that my aunt had passed away and feeling okay about it. She had fought cancer for years and was a very strong woman. It was just her time to leave the physical world and join those on the other side.

I had a long day at work and proceeded home around five o'clock. When entering my car, I looked down and noticed I had a couple of missed phone calls. I listened to the voice messages, and one was from my sister, asking me to call her. After returning home, I called my sister, and before she could say anything, I asked her if our aunt had passed away today. She said, "Oh, did someone already call you?"

I didn't have the energy to explain to her what had happened to me and just said, "Oh, yeah." We talked for a few minutes about our aunt. Knowing that she wasn't in any more pain from the cancer gave us a sense of peace about her passing. For days I wrestled with the idea of calling her children and letting them know that their mother had shown up in my arena. I didn't know if it would upset them or comfort them.

It was a Saturday morning, and I was sitting in my living room having a cup of coffee. The memories of my mother and her sister who had just passed from cancer were very strong in my mind. I reminisced about childhood days when my mother and I would often go over to my aunt's home, and I would sit and play with my cousins while my mother and her sister would sit in the kitchen and talk for hours. Knowing that my mother and aunt were together once again on the other side comforted me that day.

About a week later I was off to another horse show. During the drive I was still wrestling with the idea of calling my cousins to let them know what had happened a couple of weeks earlier. Finally I decided to go ahead and call my cousin. He's a few years younger than I am and is a very successful lawyer. I hadn't talked to him since my mother's funeral. He was surprised to hear my voice, and I asked if this was a good time to talk. He said it was and asked how I was doing. We made small talk, and I told him that I had something to share with him.

I began my story about my vision of his mother. I told him that at promptly 11 a.m. I was in my car checking for my phone messages. I had put my phone back down and looked up to get out of my car when a clear vision of his mother standing with her back to me appeared about thirty feet ahead of my car. I explained to him how she had insisted that I notice that she was bending one leg over and over. I clearly understood what she was doing, and at that point she knelt to the ground.

My cousin then stopped me and asked what time this experience had occurred. I answered eleven o'clock California time. He said that was interesting, as it would have been one o'clock North Dakota time. He explained that he was in the Bismarck hospital at one o'clock that day, standing by his mother's bedside. At one o'clock one of her legs came up off of the bed in a bent fashion. His mother was in deep sleep at that point, and he gently tried to push her leg back flat on the bed, but without success. He didn't try to push it down again and instead just gently put the covers back over her leg. He said that lasted for about thirty seconds, and then her leg went down slowly to the bed.

The similarities between what had happened in California in my vision and what had happened to him in person in a Bismarck, North Dakota hospital were amazing. He said that soon after her leg lowered back to the bed, his mother passed away. I wasn't surprised when he told me that, because it was at that point that I was watching her stand up after greeting her son and granddaughter and they all walked away hand in hand. It made sense to me that she had passed away in the hospital at that same point when her leg lowered to the bed. It was then that she crossed over and was greeted by her loved ones. My cousin was taken aback by the story and was speechless.

I went on to tell him about that Saturday morning a couple of weeks back when I was having strong memories of my mother and my aunt visiting for hours. My cousin then shared with me how on that same Saturday he was having very strong thoughts about his mother along the same pattern as mine. He was reminiscing how he would as a small boy sit in the kitchen at the table where his mother and my mother would sit and drink coffee for hours and visit. He said it was very odd that he had not had any coffee that morning, yet he had retained a strong taste of coffee in his mouth. He very rarely drank coffee, and it was odd to him that that morning the taste of coffee was so strong in his mouth. We were both overwhelmed, and we hung up feeling very happy about what had just happened for both of our families.

In trying to understand why this situation had happened to me, I didn't try to analyze it very long. I just knew that it was something once again that was supposed to happen. I am very grateful and feel very blessed that these things continue to happen in my life. And I never feel ashamed or embarrassed to share those with anyone, as it provides comfort to those who are willing to listen and open their minds.

Six years after my mother's death, my brother's son, Jared, decided to move into the farmhouse. It was our parents' dream to have the next generation grow up in the home. My mother had constantly spoken about how she wanted my brother's son to eventually live there. The time had come that my nephew was ready to take the leap. I couldn't have been happier with his decision. My sister Char and I decided to take a trip back home to help him spruce up the old farmhouse. We were very excited about going back and helping him.

We arrived at the farmhouse and were surprised by the amount of work that was already completed. New carpet and linoleum had been put down throughout the home, and the kitchen cabinets were already sanded and re-stained. There was still a lot of work to be done, and we started in by painting and putting baseboards down in all of the rooms. We worked nonstop for four days, and it turned out beautiful. My nephew was so grateful for all the work that we had done. It felt good to help with the changes, knowing that the next generation was going to be living and growing up in that house.

The time came to get back to California. It felt different leaving the ranch knowing that it had changed so much. Even though it looked beautiful and updated, it just felt different. About three days after arriving home, I received a text from my nephew living in the farmhouse. He wanted to share something with me and asked me to call when it was convenient. I called him back right after reading the text.

He said he was in the kitchen one morning doing dishes, and he felt a strong presence in the room. He felt very calm but knew something was happening. The microwave turned on by itself. He looked over at the microwave, and it shut off. He said he began to have a strong feeling that Grandma might be in the room. He said, "Grandma, is that you?" When he acknowledged the possibility that Grandma was in fact there, the microwave came back on and flashed 222 on its display. He knew at that moment that Grandma's energy and spirit were in the kitchen with him. A sense of peace came over him.

Later in the day my nephew's fiancée was walking through their bedroom, which used to be Grandma's, and as she walked by the television, it turned on. She thought it was very odd and turned it off. Later that evening when the two of them were in the bedroom, the television once again came on by itself. Just as I did, they felt that Grandma's energy was around and she was very pleased about the outcome with the farmhouse. I feel the 222 that showed up on the microwave was my mom's way of telling those in the house that not only she but Grandpa as well were very pleased with the way things had turned out. The two of them were very happy that the next generation was in the home.

After my nephew told me all of this, I was quite ecstatic knowing that my mother and father's energy and spirit were still with us. As I write this, it has been six years since my mother passed away and thirty-two years since my father passed. The energy does not dissipate. And every single one of us can have these wonderful experiences as I have had, if we just keep our eyes open and stay awake.

Chapter Sixteen

Speaking the Truth
Gives You Strength

Every now and then my mind drifts back to the evening my father visited. I now understand that he came to me in the night when all was quiet to prepare me, not for life in general, but for Mother's departure. He was always a man of few words, and the words he spoke that night have stayed with me all through the years. And he was right. It has been okay.

I have shared my experience privately and in small and large groups since that day I came back from the other side. Thus far the response has been peace, relief and happiness. I do not second guess the guidance of truth any longer; it's a feeling that is too strong. Whatever someone might imagine as "the best time ever"—nothing could ever compare to this place we go when we pass on. Call it "heaven" or something else. That alone makes living such an amazing and worthwhile gift for the time we are here. We are all here for a reason. The place where we go after the physical world, through the light, is more unbelievably wonderful than one can possibly imagine.

I am often amazed at the recounting of the event, because it feels as though I am taken back to the exact time and space that it occurred, as clear as if it had happened yesterday, even years later. I catch myself in the memory of the blessing, being allowed to go there early—a sneak peek of sorts. It seems so unreal that I am left thinking, What happened to me? Why was I the one to take my mother to the other side? Such a place of peace, where only truth and love exists. Still, I know there is a reason for us all to be here at this time—and it's for the good, not as a punishment, or a time to prove our worthiness, as some have suggested.

Even though the experience is as clear as a bell, the first year back was quite a struggle for me. I longed to be back in that energy of unconditional love. I could tell that there were people who wanted to hear the account of my experience, and I shared willingly and happily. At each accounting I felt my being becoming even more illuminated and filled with the light of heaven. I committed myself to sharing what I know with as many people as possible.

We need the peace and understanding from knowing that this really is a natural experience. To see my mother so serene and happy after so many years of discomfort brings tears to my eyes, even years later. And knowing that this is planned for all of us makes my heart leap. The ability to come back and be able to share with others—even with the limited vocabulary we have at this point—to describe the love and peace I felt while I was there, I consider a great blessing and an honor. This is especially true because on this side we are so busy, many of us have lost sight and memory of what we truly are—an expression of love; guardians of it really.

Further, I know I am not alone in the hardship of having to make that very challenging decision of life and death. People have to face it every day, and I feel for each of them, having experienced myself the remorse and questions that come with that. There are people at this moment struggling to decide the fate of a loved one. Life support serves a purpose that can be miraculous in itself. However, the decision of life and death weighs heavily upon all who must consider removing it. Even when we feel certain decisions are best for a loved one, the experience can be emotionally devastating.

However, I know without question that there is no death as we perceive it. It is just a different expression of living. Though it's difficult to adequately describe, that place we go has a feeling of what true reality is meant to be—while sometimes this life expression in a body can feel confusing and hard. Having this experience has brought me back to the understanding that we are focusing as a population on aspects of living that only hamper what our positive experience could be. It really is possible to experience heaven on earth; we just have to understand that it's possible and leave the concept of lack and scarcity behind.

I know there may be many who doubt my experience, just as I know there are others who have experienced the other side. I tell you all, I do understand. Be gentle with yourselves and with others as possibilities are explored. Keep judgment at bay. The beauty is that you have the opportunity to question anything in this life, to investigate, to study. It's okay. Such actions develop faith. Even this part of the human experience is a gift, and I find it very reassuring. You will find out for yourself when the time comes, so enjoy, be kind, love, and share while you are here! Even though I may not personally know you, I find great joy knowing that you will be welcomed and loved beyond your comprehension.

We are to love people wholly and experience with them. They must continue their path as you must—you will see them again. When I examine the major events in my life, the ones that stand out for some reason, I see there has been a driving force delivering me right here, in front of you, even though I was completely unaware at the time. I invite you to do the same and see if you can see this for yourself.

There is a reason you are reading this book right now. Maybe you need to release fear about that part of life we call death. Maybe you need peace in your life about letting someone else go. Maybe you need to know that there really is a reason for you to be here and to know that you are very loved and protected.

Focus on joy, and others will catch on. It is all waiting for you. The reasons it happened this way, to me, still elude me. I only know that I came back willingly and with a grateful heart in the knowledge of what waits for us, and to share this with you. We buy into so much fear. It can all be a joyous time depending on how we focus our attention. Until my time finally comes—which I will look forward to—I'm staying awake.